ken

...ity Education
An Account of the Liverpool Project

Eric Midwinter

Eric Midwinter was born and educated at Sale, near Manchester.

A scholar of St Catharine's College, Cambridge, where he graduated in 1955 with First Class Honours in the Historical Tripos, he subsequently gathered an M.A. in Education at Liverpool and a Doctorate at York University with a thesis on those Victorian social issues which have contributed so much to the present problems of Educational Priority Areas. After a career mainly in teacher-education, he became Director of the Liverpool Educational Priority Area Project, 1968–71. Since January of 1972 he has been Director of Priority, a national centre in Liverpool for urban community education and itself both a continuation and an extension of the Liverpool EPA Project. He is the Co-Director of the Advisory Centre for Education, Cambridge, and he acts as Educational Consultant to the Home Office Community Development Projects. His other books include, *Social Administration in Lancashire, 1830–1860, Victorian Social Reform, Nineteenth Century Education, Projections: An EPA Project at Work*, and *Social Environment and the Urban School*.

Aged forty, married with two children, he is an unrepentant supporter of Manchester United and Lancashire County Cricket Club and has a strong but, he hopes, not allied interest in English music hall comedy.

Priority Education
An Account of the Liverpool Project
Eric Midwinter

Penguin Books

Penguin Books Ltd, Harmondsworth,
Middlesex, England
Penguin Books Inc., 7110 Ambassador Road,
Baltimore, Md 21207, USA
Penguin Books Australia Ltd,
Ringwood, Victoria, Australia

First published 1972
Copyright © Eric Midwinter, 1972

Made and printed in Great Britain by
Cox & Wyman Ltd,
London, Reading and Fakenham
Set in Intertype Plantin

For Margaret

Contents

Preface   9

1 **The Solution**
The Community School   11

2 **The Situation**
Liverpool's Educational Priority Area   26

3 **The Method**
The Technique of Action Research   46

4 **The Approach**
Building a Team and a Programme   58

5 **The Action 1**
The Project at Work   79

6 **The Action 2**
Four Case Studies   133

7 **The Conclusion**
The Urban Community School   160

8 **The Future**
Too Little, Too Late?   186

Preface

This book is based on the energy and inventiveness of everyone associated with the Liverpool Education Priority Area Project. I owe them an enormous professional and personal debt, and, hopefully, most of them have been appreciatively noted in the text. I have thoroughly enjoyed the support of a loyal and gifted team, a sympathetic and imaginative Steering Committee, a generous and hospitable local authority and, in Chelly Halsey, an always encouraging and stimulating National Director. The book, of course, is really for and about the teachers, children and parents of Liverpool's EPA schools, who, in the most difficult circumstances, gave unselfishly and unstintingly for the furtherment of our work. It is written in the hope that, for them and their fellows elsewhere, social justice will out.

Jonathan Croall and Richard Mabey of Penguin have been models of heartening comment and discreet suggestion, and, finally, a warm word of thanks to my secretary, Jill West, for so cheerfully and competently helping me to beat the publishing clock.

1 The Solution
The Community School

Educational priority areas: The question raised

The national EPA project arose from the Plowden Report's concern with 'the seamless web of circumstance', 'the cumulative deprivation' and 'the ingrained dirt of generations' which characterized certain underprivileged areas. In particular, the report recommended that 'research should be started to discover which of the developments in Educational Priority Areas have the more constructive effects, so as to assist in planning the longer term programme to follow.'* Accordingly, grants amounting to £175,000 were awarded by the Department of Education and Science and the Social Sciences Research Council for action-research in a number of areas. Dr Michael Young, Chairman of the Institute of Urban Studies, was appointed Chairman of the National EPA Steering Committee, and Dr A. H. Halsey, Head of the Oxford University Department of Social and Administrative Studies, was appointed National Director. Oxford University was to serve as the national headquarters of the project. After a series of negotiations, Liverpool was chosen as one of five areas for the project, along with Denaby in the West Riding, the Deptford area of London, and Balsall Heath in Birmingham, with Dundee enjoying a slightly differing relationship administratively. As with the other areas, the local LEA and University were intrinsically involved in the exercise.

The remit for the action-research in selected EPAs outlined the aims as four fold. These were to raise educational standards, to lift teacher-morale, to solder home and school links and to assist in giving communities a sense of responsibility. 'What,' asked a colleague, 'do you do in the second week?'

* Central Advisory Council for Education (England), *Children and Their Primary Schools* (The Plowden Report), 1967, vol. 1, ch. 5 paras. 131–3, 173 and 177.

It was not simply that this was a somewhat lofty series of goals for a two-man team and a three-year project. Each of the aims also begged the question: were the standards low and were the right standards being applied; were the teachers demoralized or, at least, more so than their suburban counterparts; were all home–school links so desirable and were they to be teacher – or parent – orientated; to which community should responsibility be engendered and for what purpose? These, and a dozen other queries, emphasized the vague and ambiguous nature of the aims.

Faced with the sheer hard fact of social deprivation, one could hardly escape the view that equality of opportunity was, without equality of conditions, a sham. Home circumstances were obviously critical and those, in turn, were adversely related to class and neighbourhood patterns. The school where, after all, the children spent only five hours of the day, seemed comparatively powerless to alter matters radically of its own volition. Assuredly, a decision, nationally taken by the EPA projects, to consider the EPA school in its communal setting was a wise one, and the Plowden Committee had been well-advised to recommend that community schools should be developed in all areas but especially in EPAs.*

This much agreed, at least within the project teams, there still remained the question of what the solution was. It was, and is, commonly felt that a discriminatory boost was needed in the backward areas to bring education up to scratch so that, for instance, the thousands leaving school at fifteen who had the potential to benefit from advanced schooling might stay on. The Plowden Report argued this respectable and widely held thesis with admirable spirit. It detailed a programme of 'positive discrimination' and 'a new distribution of educational resources', through priority building and minor works, improved staffing and auxiliary help, supplemented salaries and so on. This was designed to cater for 'a great reservoir of unrealized potential', for 'what these deprived areas need most are perfectly normal good primary schools.' Twice over Plowden decreed that the EPA schools should be as good as the best in the land.†

* *Plowden*, op. cit., ch. 4 para. 130 vii, and ch. 5 para. 167.
† *Plowden*, op. cit., ch. 5, especially paras. 136–52 and 158–73.

The suspicion that this view was misleading grew, during the early months of the project, into a gravely nagging doubt. Because the normal educational system failed to operate efficiently in every single area across the nation, it was supposed that a more varied imposition of that system would help close, to quote Plowden again, 'the gap between the educational opportunities of the most and least fortunate children ... for economic and social reasons alike.' We wondered whether an alternative explanation was worthy of consideration. Perhaps having a uniform system was wrong. Perhaps different sorts of areas required different educational systems.

The irrelevance of the curriculum

The educational servicing of a multivariant society with a singular system leads to schools which fail to relate to the experience of their pupils and their catchment area. Often, it would appear, the curriculum is irrelevant to the community, its children and both their needs. One might embark on a mental journey through a school day. Ten years of college of education tutorship warned me off visiting any primary school between 9.30 and 10.30. They're almost always doing maths: when the children are 'fresh', according to the theory, as if other branches of academy didn't require quick wits and could safely be postponed until the afternoon. Every day the compulsory act of worship is followed by the equally sacramental celebration of holy maths. There is the ancient – A, B and C filling that leaky bath, – and there is the modern – a student I knew, in an effort at making her sums 'concrete', asked the children to calculate seven-eighths of 7,640 ... grapes! Whichever it is, is there not just too much of it for children whose major problems in life are social ones. Ever since that dangerously simple slogan 'the three Rs' was enunciated, maths has been second in the timetable's top of the pops, pushing English for the number one spot. Latterly, the mathematicians – who seem to enjoy the most superb public relations techniques in education – dreamed up 'modern' maths and coined 'numeracy' to set against 'literacy', another deceptively innocuous word that somehow suggests the two are in equal quantities and should be similarly treated.

This fundamental lack of reappraisal of school subjects

continues throughout the day. Methods have changed but not, in the same proportion, content. The tune changes but the melody lingers on. College tutors can pull another little trick by telling students the age of a class by the history they do: seven year olds doing Ancient Britons and Romans; eight year olds doing monks and manors, and so on. Often Richard Lionheart will now be 'done', not by chalk and talk, but in project form, with booklets, ribbons and, if an article falls conveniently, a scissored assault on the colour supplements. But it's still Richard Lionheart – and, given only a short time in school and dreadful problems to face, is it strictly useful to know about a homosexual, absentee feudal monarch?

I recall making much the same point to a group of students about geography, a discipline which sometimes seems to attract more and more attention to items as they grow less and less meaningful. The Eskimoes were the case at hand; not only were they remote from the child's experience, many of them now, far from living, blubber-bound, in igloos, wear suits and man American bases. One of the students went into a school next day and the teacher said: 'you can do the Eskimoes; I've been saving them all year, because I know students like to do them'.

Even reading, the citadel of primary education, is open to criticism. The frequently astringent debate over which reading method to employ has apparently allowed reading to become an end rather than a means. To teach reading without purpose is, arguably, to make children more vulnerable to the ad-mass and to give them a kind of narcotic to help them through the bad times. Perhaps Janet and John are drug-pushers, with reading replacing religion as the opium of the people.

But apart from the irrelevance of the content and the lack of social purpose, there is the straight educational or psychological question – can the children understand it? If, as most commentators accept, the conceptual grasp of the child grows, like his physical and other features, then a child-centred education should eschew that which the child cannot conceive of nor, in some fashion, experience. The Masai Tribe is outside his spatial and the Anglo-Saxons are outside his temporal frame of reference: both stump him in terms of political and social concepts.

Much schoolwork is as remote from understanding as from experience, simply because the two are intimately interwoven. There is that neutered quartet who ineluctably figure in every set of readers – daddy, mummy, brother, sister, all impeccably mannered and irritatingly cheerful as, with the unavoidable Rover, they assiduously pursue their tedious round of days in the country, visits to the seaside, journeys to the farm and tours of the shops, from the secure base of their nineteen-thirties suburb.

No wonder we get schoolboy howlers. Presented with information divorced from experience, children strive to connect it with the most approximate reality. Some time ago I inspected a child's drawing of 'Silent Night; Holy Night'. As well as the traditional complement of holy family, wise men, shepherds, oxen and asses, there was also a cheerful, stout fellow in a brown jerkin gazing benignly into the crib. 'Who is that?' we asked. 'Round John Virgin', said the artist. We compound the felony. At the end of a day's journey through a school timetable, one might summarily conclude not only that much of the substance taught was useless to the child, but that he couldn't understand it properly anyway!

An unfair caricature, of course; cruelly unfair to hundreds of engaged and penetrating teachers, but it catches some of the remoteness of school-content today. Conservation is, for several reasons, probably stronger in education than in most other national institutions. The subject divisions and much of their contents are still, arguably, of Victorian origin and before. They match an austerely sterile trait with a quashily romanticist style. They were never very real; now they are far removed in time and mood from everyday life. This makes unwitting hypocrites of teachers. They talk of Francis Drake, and then hide him away, without another thought, until his turn comes around next year; the only children who 'use' him are those who become teachers. They read Victorian poesy to the children and extoll the virtues of rural life, only to return to their centrally-heated city houses to watch 'Coronation Street' on telly. Even the futuristic discipline, science, which, with its Botto-gas jars, is descending into the primary schools, that the technological revolution be nigh, is musty, tweedy and redolent of the South Kensington Science Museum at the turn of the century.

Perhaps the spectacular changes in schools have blinkered educationists into a belief that fundamental change has occurred. The major change, in the physical condition and treatment of children, is no more than a reflection of twentieth century social values, welcome although it obviously is. The minor change has been in method, and teachers have seen, in altered method, educational revolution. But balderdash is not changed by transferring it from blackboard to tape-recorder, nor is rubbish transposed by its being taught informally rather than formally. If a piece of teaching is an arrant nonsense then the change from slip-tests in serried ranks arrayed to discovery by hanging from the chandeliers will not make it sane.

To some degree the educational battle between 'idealists' and 'realists' or 'progressives' and 'traditionalists' is like the Large-enders and Small-enders in Gulliver's Lilliput. Neither side concerns itself with the egg, but only how to crack it. The point is most alarmingly to be found in the field of modern languages. Despite the blandishments of the Common Market, we really must face the reality that, in terms of educational priorities, the average child's need for any foreign language, least of all French, is not very pressing. Today, with its battery of language laboratories and tape-recorders, French has invaded the primary school, and the old classicist's jibe about turning out children illiterate in two languages is near to fruition. At a time when proportionately fewer people take holidays in France, the press report of Princess Margaret opening a primary school in Barrow and 'during the Princess' visit not one word of English was spoken' is tragi-comic. Yet now, schools are judged 'good' if they include a modern language in the curriculum. When children in Barrow are not talking English, the divorcement of school from community is complete!

Empirically, one sees, not so much people in literary or numerary difficulty, as in social difficulty, for which the schools have done insufficient to prepare them. One walks about Liverpool for hours waiting for someone to ask for a simultaneous equation to be solved, or for 'If I were Lord of Tartary' to be recited. However, the synthetic heritage that the education system passes on to children can be important. The child who can remember and regurgitate the algebraic formulae, the industries of Upper Silesia, the character-studies of Brutus and Cassius, the campaigns of Marlborough and the domestic life of the field-mouse has five 'O' levels, and bids fair to pass through sixth form to college or university. Herein lie some, at least, of the keys to the materialist treasures of Western society. It is a daunting and ironic thought that the memorization of such a sterile hotch-potch might lead to the semi-detached, car-owning spoils of competitive commercial life.

The need for social education

Granted some truth in this impressionistic view of English education, this thinking on paper around a gnawing doubt, how does it affect the EPA? Simply, success in the middle-class school is the norm, so that the game, however ludicrous, is no more than amusing. In the EPA school, where failure is the norm, it is black comedy. The opportunity is equal; the dimensions of the pitch and the rules of the game are similar, but some of the competitors are nobbled.

Several commentators have pointed to the trials of working-class children mounting the educational ladder. In the application of a uniform system throughout the nation, it is possible to note the inculcation of what, in a shorthand phrase, may be called bourgeois values. For historical and other reasons, the schools and their operators have something of a middle-class orientation. This means that the middle-class child finds in the school an extension of his home, and the EPA child discovers, to some extent, a rejection of his home. It is not too polemical to imply that, to the injury of a deprived existence, is added the insult of an alien educational system.

These points are raised as philosophic queries. Is the curriculum of the EPA school relevant to its children's needs? Are the values of the EPA school suitable for its children's social adjustment? Of one thing we may be sure. Education success for the EPA child might be measured in terms of escape from his depressing habitat to the white picket fences and pleasing lawns of Wallasey and Southport. And, it must immediately be added, no one would deny them the chance. By lubricating the creaking machinery of EPA education, more potential might well be realized à la Plowden, with more early leavers staying on for higher education. At best, however, this would still leave a slightly diluted majority to face the rigours of what might prove to be lifelong deprivation.

In 1991 the population of Liverpool's inner ring will be 73,000 or so, the planners predict. Many of the children in our project schools will have children of their own at school by then. It is unlikely that the 73,000 will mainly be sales representatives, managers and even school teachers. It is more likely that many will fall into the nineteen-nineties equivalent of classes 4 and 5 on the Occupational Register. It is not quite 'Alice in Wonderland', where everyone won a prize. There are likely, even with greatly improved facilities in education as it stands, to be more losers than winners, for, in the last analysis, there is simply not room for everyone in the higher socio-economic grades. It struck us that, while obviously remembering the needs of local boys with the latent talent to make good, our preoccupation should be with the huge majority who will live forever in the deprived area.

Their housing will doubtless improve physically, as the municipal rehousing exercise evolves. Teachers, however, seem as troubled by children from the new as from the antiquated housing, and the evidence of educational advancement on outlying municipal estates is not too encouraging. This might well be because of dislocation and because the bureaucrat presumably believes that people are automatically happier in a sterile, hygenic unit than in a cosy unsanitary home. The point, convincingly made by J. W. B. Douglas, that parental interest is more significant in education attainment than type of neighbourhood may be of import here. It may also be that a purely physical transmission does not necessarily evince a divine metamorphosis. Long term prisoners, transferred from the ancient dungeons of Durham to their spanking new security wing on the Isle of Wight, still remain long-term prisoners.

One difficulty is that the suburban model is, in practice, the only model both for builder and resident, so that municipal housing often palely apes the flat or the semi-detached house of suburbia. There seems neither the scope nor the creative spark to revitalize and rebuild city life in a novel image, to conjoin, as it were, twentieth century amenities with a Renaissance spirit. It is difficult to believe that, of itself, hot water running in carefully planned council flats will enliven an interest in education. As it is, one might fear that social composition is becoming more and not less polarized, as the wage-earners gravitate to the rented municipal estates and the salary-earners to the mortgaged owner-occupied private estates. Come comprehensive schools and sixth form colleges, that curious compound of academic recognition and vocational status which has come to be labelled 'meritocratic' partly draws in the dividing line. In Liverpool, we call this the Wimpey-Skem syndrome.

The alternative might be to offer the majority of children a social education; one that might give them the social competences to examine the depressing reality of their world, in the hope that they might learn to repair or change it in ways agreeable and pleasing to them. Through a close investigation of their social environment, the children might be that much readier to understand their own needs with more clarity. From that standpoint, they might come to invent ways and means of satisfying those needs. This is the opposite of persuading children to resign themselves stoically to their lot. This is an attempt to make them think and act boldly and inventively about their lot. What it does not do is pretend the lot is necessarily a happy one. One hopes to replace resignation and negative rebelliousness with a positive reformist attitude.

Such an open-ended investigation of the social environment (not just, let it be noted, the *local* environment: for example: television and advertising are non-local forces in the children's environment) might be the foundation of the EPA Community School. There would be an attempt to tap the potential and the experience of the city child in his own right, with rather less of that escapism with which teachers have superficially attempted to polish the urban child. It has been as though they wanted to paint a quick-dry cultural gloss on to the pupil. The social environmentally-based curriculum is psychologically more accurate. It begins with the child's experience and works purposefully *outwards*. So much teaching of the urban child has, in the past, postulated new experiences without lifelines from the old.

Such a radical re-think of the EPA syllabus would, of course, require many changes in the structure of the school and of teaching and it would imply a much more exciting and intimate re-

lation of the school to its catchment area. It means long looks at
the school's situation vis-à-vis many social institutions, the most
prominent of these being, naturally enough, the home. But the
other social and economic amenities around the school must also
be introduced into and related to the exercise, so that the school
might become the hub of a thriving, socially-based educational
process, rather than the exclusive and sometimes withdrawn
agency of education.

The hypothesis was ill-defined and somewhat vague because it
was raised pensively as a question and because it threw up additional problems rather than reassuring solutions. The outline
proposed here is deliberately a paraphrase of an early brief and it
properly indicates the hesitancy and anxiety of those initial discussions. Others were confidently aiming to increase verbal skills
or some other accepted educational skill. We began with a
question-mark against our goal. Our random thoughts offered no
more than a teaching question. In brief, should the EPA Community School concern itself rather more with things of immediate relevance than with the siren calls of academic successes in a
misty future?

The community school and community action

The possible implications for the project's four stated aims were
substantial. If the educational standards of the EPA school were
not low but wrong, might it not be that teacher morale suffered
because their expectation followed suit? In other words, perhaps
teachers felt depressed that their charges looked feeble in com-
parison with middle-class pupils, and that, consequently, a suitable adjustment of syllabus and approach might encourage
teachers beneficially. Further, the ravages of parental alienation
might in part be repaired. Almost by definition, EPA parents are
school 'failures', who had probably disliked school intensely. It has
been competently argued that the attempt to generate interest
among parents is highly difficult and that new teaching methods
may have led to a greater exclusion of the working-class parent
from the child's school experience. The most well-intentioned
schools may, therefore, be attempting, if their structure is un-
changed, to be selling what to the parents is a bad product twice.
It is almost as though, subconsciously, the parents accept that

school-life and real-life are poles apart, and that involvement is a wasteful exercise. Given a school system more realistically related to the community, might some of this alien feeling be relieved? Similarly with communal responsibility; the community might just assimilate the school a little more fluidly (and, of course, move a little to meet the school) if its character were more obviously aligned with communal mores.

On this analysis, the chief meaning of the Plowden Report was to assert roundly that so-called equal opportunity left untouched areas of significant underprivilege. The Report said: ' "Equality" has an appealing ring; "discrimination" has not.'* This was as brave and as important a statement as the earlier proposition of equality of opportunity which had, of course, proved an ethical as well as a social improvement. Plowden gave an opportunity to inspect this fine ideal against several years of empirical practice. Where Plowden may have been slightly misleading was in its suggestion that 'compensation' would automatically result in betterment. It left unsaid what appeared to be a possible logical consequence of the EPA premise: namely, that EPA schools should, in their very nature and provision, be different from non-EPA schools and that EPA teachers should, in part, have specific EPA education for their role. This was said grudgingly by a project team nurtured, as teachers, in the idea of professional unity, but, logically, there must be repercussions in teacher-training if the EPA school is to alter either at base or in superstructure. Just as, in teacher-education, there are chronological variations between junior and secondary trainees, there might have to be sociological variations, possibly by second or third year option, between EPA, suburban and other groups of students.

This viewpoint does no disservice to the pioneers who campaigned for parity of opportunity. They doubtless imagined that equality of opportunity would beget conditions in which forthcoming generations would automatically start at par. This has not, unhappily, transpired. Those working in a deprived area find the alarums and the postures of the Black Paper anti-egalitarian commentators laughable. They shout before they are hurt. One might recall the words of one of those veteran educational thinkers, R. H. Tawney: of the nation's children, he wrote '. . . if,

* *Plowden,* op. cit, ch. 5 para. 148.

instead of rejuvenating the world, they grind corn for the Phil-
istines and doff bobbins for the mill-owners, the responsibility is
ours into whose hands the prodigality of nature pours life
itself.'* Eventually, an EPA community must stand on its own
feet like any other and rejuvenate its world, and that is a dogma
which might hold good on both political wings, for the right
wing in English politics has its commitments to local autonomy
and individual self-help, just as the left wing is devoted to the
pursuit of social justice.

The Community School, then, emphasizes the differences
rather than the similarities of schools precisely because it attempts to relate fluently and productively with the ethos, character and values of the community it serves. This is what makes it a
relevant school. By establishing school-community inter-
connections, it constructs a stable basis upon which a three-
cornered partnership of parent, teacher and child might
harmoniously operate. The Community School ventures out into
the community. The Community School welcomes in the community. Ideally, the barriers would collapse completely and the
borders become indistinguishably blurred. Physically, one
might foresee a time when, architecturally, the school, along with
all other social agencies, might be subsumed into the community.
The shopping precinct prampark might run into the nursery
unit; the school clinic and the civic group surgery might be one;
and the children might eat their school dinner in what is also the
local café and snack-bar.

Gone would be the seclusion of the traditional English school,
with children drawn in and instructed behind closed doors and
high walls. The Community School requires a highly socialized
format because it has a social rather than an academic aim. Its
long-term purpose is to equip the critical parent, worker, consumer and citizen of the next generation, in the hope that that
generation might respond creatively to the challenge of deprivation. It is an attempt to break the poverty cycle, in which
deprived parents have bred deprived children in deprived situations to become, in turn, the deprived parents of deprived children. It is an attempt to replace the ad hoc sporadic

*R. H. Tawney, *The Acquisitive Society*, 1921, Bell, republished 1961,
p. 81.

governmental palliatives with a fullrun policy of self-renewal and community revitalization.

As such, it turns the traditional school approach on its head. The school has always been a relatively uninfluential agency for social change. It is an affirming mechanism. It is not going to Eton or to St Pancras RC Primary in Braddersfield that transforms you into an overemployed cabinet minister or an unemployed cabinet maker; it is being born into that particular avenue of life in which Eton or St Pancras stands and which you experience as you pass down the avenue. This is the lesson of the home and school researchers. It is home and neighbourhood that is important; the school merely accepts and confirms.

Willy nilly, schools have tended to defend the status quo, and there are countless social and professional pressures upon teachers to continue this hundreds-year-old convention. But, in our deprived urban districts, it is the status quo that is wrong. The Community needs to be changed and thus the Community School has to be involved in changing and not in standing still. Teachers will have to become social prosecutors rather than social defenders, if the school is, in effect, to shift itself massively and become a positive influence on social change.

It is immediately obvious that the school cannot operate alone, and here one meets one of the first golden rules of the Community School; namely, one cannot have community education without community development and one cannot have community development without community education. It would be, on the one hand, frustrating to turn out a sane, critical, well-balanced product, eager for the participatory democracy fray, only to find that participatory democracy – in the workplace, on the streets, over local issues, in the shops and so on – was absent. It would, on the other hand, be wasteful to create a grassroots community organism, if the people had not been given the opportunity to develop the essential social skills for its most fruitful usage. The planner, paying his lipservice to consultation, knocks on the door and asks the client what sort of home or environment he would like. The answer should properly be: 'I was never educated to hear that question; I was never educated to articulate an answer; if you'd like me to tell you about Who Flung, the little Chinese boy, a day in the life of Egbert, the little Anglo-Saxon boy or the story of Tobias, the little boy who knew St Paul, come round in the morning and we'll give it a whirl'.

Community education should provide an important servicing agency for community development, ensuring that, if all the elements – law and order, housing, welfare, transport, social and utility services – are drawn into a unified communal enterprise, its patrons would be well-versed in how to cope with the operation. Children in school should be, in A. H. Halsey's compelling phrase, 'eager apprentices for community life'. Community education for the socially disadvantaged should be part of the gamut of community development for the socially disadvantaged. Perhaps, indeed, it should be first among equals. It is increasingly apparent that, of itself, education cannot compensate for the malpractices and injustices of society. It can contribute, but it can only contribute profitably in a propitious community clime.

The community module is no stranger to political science. Aristotle anticipated us for one. It has respectable medieval and nineteenth century antecedents. Now it is the task of the community developer to modify the ideal of autarchy to twentieth century conditions and, assuredly, education has a significant role to play. The community educationist is at once more long-sighted and more pessimistic than the compensatory educationist. He looks far beyond the short-term blandishments of an improved reading age to the sunny vision of a highly skilled citizenry recreating high quality civic life in our cities. In so doing he notes, at base, that education cannot go it alone – he is not, then, optimistic about the school as a kind of Lone Ranger solving all educational and thereby social problems, with the silver bullets of language programmes and numeracy drives. To hack at a fearful metaphor, this particular Lone Ranger would need a number of Tontoes to be guarding the flanks of all the other social factors in civic life.

Of course, it is a spiral process. It is not a question of solving problems independently. Community education does not have to be perfected, it need only be well under way, to provoke articulate and valid pressures for reform through an improved utilization of existing possibilities; as reforms in other spheres are accomplished, the confidence in and investment in community education could grow, and so on. For example, a more socially aware community could use the existing channels of social welfare benefits or the existing avenues of political protest with increased skill. This, in turn, might bring about alterations in welfare administration or an acquaintance with political techniques (such as school management) and both could visibly affect the everyday life of the Community School.

There is a circular argument surrounding the promulgation of democracy. Can the individual be trusted to exercise democratic power fully or must he be content with his quintennial excursion to the polling station; if he be given sovereign power, will the efficiency and productivity of our society be undermined because of his lack of know-how and his insufficiency of responsibility? We tend to keep democracy at arm's length or, rather, at ballot-box length. It seems we cannot afford the risk of popular as opposed to constitutional democracy; naturally, the only way to discover the truth of the argument is to give it a try, but we flinch from this. In terms of the schools, there are many ready to argue that we should leave well alone and tamper but gently with a reasonably effective system which produces a modicum of scientists, doctors, engineers and clergymen. Parents, it is still argued, would be in the way and would not be expert enough to join in a total discussion about their own children's futures.

Here is the crux. It is the age-old state versus individual dilemma. But the state is an aggregate of individuals. As for the state education system, it is a remarkable illustration of the point, for – as community developers have been quick to observe – it is the highest common multiple of community development. Everyone has been to school; many have children at school; education should and could be a lifelong process; everyone lives near to and recognizes the school as an ongoing social agency; ratepayers and taxpayers both fork out mightily for it. It is the goal of community education to make the state's educational system more truthfully the people's system and to deploy it more beneficially as a support and as a keystone for grassroots democracy and community involvement.

2 The Situation
Liverpool's Educational Priority Area

The growth of Liverpool's Inner Ring

'Did this happen in Liverpool?' the reporter insisted. He was pointing to a sentence in a pamphlet I'd written on teaching in Educational Priority Areas. It ran: 'this girl, a Christmas or two ago, saw her father slaughter her mother and sister with a hatchet.' I had to tell him I'd read about this tragedy in his own paper. Most people read or know about the pressures of poverty and deprivation, but so few are able to make the educational correlation. That child had, a few days later, to re-enter school and continue her education. It is an extreme case, but there are many extreme cases in an Educational Priority Area. Many are not, luckily, as horribly spectacular as this one, but one could catalogue list after list of case-histories of children whose domestic or environmental situation militates strongly against their educational chance. It was, paradoxically, the shock and glare of publicity that greeted this particular pamphlet that was so discouraging. Everyone came to talk about 'that child is dropping with fatigue because his mother, a prostitute, and her customer had first call on the bed' or 'that girl was tied up and beaten in a derelict house as a ploy in some macabre protection racket.' Did they not know that such things happened to children and that, ineluctably, they blunt the children's educational reflexes? Do people have to be luridly told, every month or so, that children are living multideprived existences, so that we can maintain some sort of pressure to put their educational problems to rights?

It is disturbing that people's – especially children's – miseries needed to be paraded constantly to stir the national conscience. Beyond that, one is never quite sure how sensitive people are to their own situation. To pursue this opening tone of depression, I once visited a new block of flats and the mothers showed me their homes. As they proudly and validly demonstrated their house-wifery, they interlaced their commentary with almost casual asides – 'we can't keep wallpaper on the walls because of the condensation'; 'we don't go out after half past six – even when the lifts are working, the lads would threaten to stick you with a knife'; 'this is Mr Jenks, the caretaker – he's burning five gallons of paraffin down the refuse shaft; someone blocked it with a piece of plywood'; 'there's urine and worse in the lift'; 'drunks smashed the adventure playground the other week, smashed it up about three o'clock in the morning'; 'they've bricked up those little bicycle sheds at the bottom – they were being used for stolen goods'. All mentioned by the by in between enthusiasm for the new paradise society had bestowed upon them after the hell of twelve years in one room on the south side of the city. Such good cheer was, again paradoxically, a depressing feature. Had these parents been really kidded into believing that their problems had been solved by the highrise panacea? How do you tell people that they or their children are, in terms of accepted life-chances, 'deprived'?

Put in this polarized form, the job of Director of an EPA Project had a bizarre cast. It was sometimes hard to convince society that it had victims and, equally, it was occasionally difficult to persuade the victims of their fate. On the one hand, 'society' was ready to complain when crime and delinquency menaced while, on the other hand, the EPA denizens were willing to criticize the corporation and all manner of authority until the cows came home. But a simple analysis of an imbalanced social system which gave unfair deals sometimes was ignored by the one and resented by the other. Certainly it stared everyone in the face, and one could only conclude that all kinds of blinkers prevented everyone seeing the social injustice implicit in the EPA problem.

It is nowhere better to be observed than on Merseyside, for the pattern of urban decay and renewal is classically demonstrated by Liverpool. Bound into a rough quadrant by the angle formed by the Mersey and its estuary, Liverpool's growth has been in radial spokes from its dockside core. As these spokes have joined together laterally, great socio-economic arcs have been created. The expansion of the port and its adjacent commercial life has

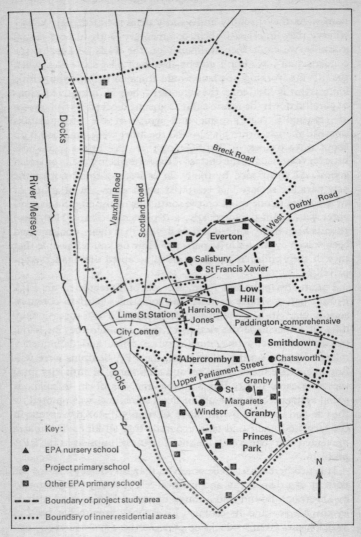

Figure 1 Liverpool County Borough: the inner areas

been, of course, the major cause of these massive social pulsations. As the business peninsula grew, so some of the working-class areas were assimilated and, alongside the tremendous demographic increases, this, in turn, led to the middle-class properties being overwhelmed. And the middle-classes edged further into the hinterland, assisted first by the railways and then by the electric trams, the buses and the motor car. One spur pressed northward. The docks pushed into Bootle, where Gladstone is reputed to 'have seen wild roses growing in the village centre', and the merchants and professional people trekked along the coast initially into Waterloo and Seaforth and then on through Crosby to Southport. A similar southern migration, fed by the ferries and eventually the Mersey Tunnel, carried the suburbs on to the Wirral which, in the eighteen-thirties, had been England's most notorious wrecking coast. Between these two, a central flange extended eastward to complete the Merseyside conurbation. It is happening again. A second Mersey Tunnel, the huge new Seaforth Dock and ribbons of motorway at the north end, and one watches the cycle gyrate: 'Deeply concerned', led the front page of *The Crosby Herald* on 3 December 1971, 'by the the dereliction which has resulted, particularly in the southern end of the borough, with the coming of the new dock at Seaforth, Crosby Council is prepared to go as far as petitioning the Prime Minister to put their case.'

Many of the working-class courts and cellar dwellings, sternly denounced for their insanitary condition by mid-nineteenth century public health reformers, mouldered where commercial premises now stand. Williamson Square was then a favourite vice spot for the sailor ashore, with its twenty or more drinking saloons, flash-houses and brothels. The Theatre Royal, noted for its riotous character, was situated there, with the galleryites often providing a dramatic highlight by urinating into the pit. Maybe they would have felt at home in the lifts of the highrise blocks. Now Williamson Square houses shops, a taxi-rank and the highly respectable Playhouse, with its brand new gleaming restaurant, and it is overlooked by two of Liverpool's leading stores. The Theatre Royal became a cold storage depot, recently demolished to make way for a car park. Conversely, the new comprehensive school, where the project had its office, was at that time fields just outside the borough boundary. Now it is near the centre of an Educational Priority Area. In a hundred and fifty years the almost Spenglerian cycle of rural outskirts, middle-class property, working-class housing and urban decay has rolled over it.

No mere antiquarian interest prompts this brief chronicling of Liverpool's social development. It is necessary to place the problem in its historical perspective, to absorb some feeling of the tempo of change to realize that the issue of educational deprivation has been two centuries in the making. Population is one guide. It rose from 5,000 to 78,000 in the eighteenth century, and then to over half a million in the nineteenth. It is now over 677,000. Of these 230,000 live in the city's inner ring. This huge curving band is sandwiched between the city centre and the long crescent of Liverpool's main suburbs, roughly following the line of the city's sweep of parks. It is its being trapped and crushed between centre and suburb that gives the inner ring its chief characteristic of social friction. It is as though a quarter of a million people have been caught up helplessly between the advancing commercial Egyptians and the fleeing suburban Israelites.

This is an oversimplification, but it suggests the essence of the problem. It should not, however, be thought that the inner ring is as neatly defined as a short description perhaps implies. The borders are extremely blurred, the social and physical characteristics are inextricably mixed and, far from being static, the area is in constant turmoil. Walk out of Liverpool centre and climb one of the mild gradients into this zone and one is never quite sure when one has entered or left it. This is possibly the first priority of the Educational Priority Area; to find, identify and nail the actual area. The grey, anonymous nature of down-town Liverpool and its sheer lack of political entity makes the task of equating education and the community doubly difficult. Nor was this helped by the varied physical structure of the area, ranging from the terraced rows of artisan housing, via the demolished sites and the suddenly towering blocks of municipal flats, to the sad run-down merchant housing of yesteryear.

The Liverpool educational priority area

Within this torn and battered swathe, some fifty primary school departments had officially been designated EPA in 1968 by the Department of Education and Science and the staffs were in receipt of an extra increment. Of these thirteen – four church school departments, the rest state schools including one nursery school – had been preselected by the local authority for initial attachment to the project. They randomly transversed the centre of the inner band and presented a useful cross-section of the area. All the schools, it must be added, were unfailingly co-operative, helpful and generous to the project team. Their catchment areas were minimally encompassed by six wards, covering much of Liverpool 7 and Liverpool 8 and touching on Liverpool 3. These six wards were Abercromby, Everton, Granby, Low Hill, Princes Park and Smithdown. Among them they rang all the social changes. Everton, from the early nineteenth century, had been an artisan quarter, albeit now refurbished sporadically with highrise dwellings. Abercromby and Princes Park had provided the Victorian middle-classes with the formal soundness of solid merchant avenues and squares, and these, for the most part, were now decaying beyond redemption. Granby had barely existed in 1870, but, in the last quarter of the century, the so-called 'byelaw housing', with its rigid terraces of rented working-class accommodation, had put it on the map. The area had samples of every developmental stage; seedy Victorian, private terraced, pre-war municipal, post-war municipal and clearance sites. By 1972 thousands of houses, upright at the beginning of the project, had been swept away.

Ironically, the study area included many of Liverpool's cultural highspots. The Philharmonic Hall and the Everyman Theatre lay within its bounds, while the rapidly extending University campus dwelt, inappropriately, right in the middle of the Educational Priority Area. A couple of colleges of education were on its outskirts, and the area also included the Regional College of Art and two or three of Liverpool's better-known secondary schools. Liverpool's two famous cathedrals looked down upon the EPA and any number of hospitals testified to this being Liverpool's traditional medical area. A brisk walk or a short bus ride would carry one from any part of the area into the bright lights of the city's shopping thoroughfares. Again, Liverpool's 'high degree of centrality' must be stressed. In 1965 one in eight of all jobs on Merseyside was in the city centre, and 26 per cent of the conurbation's retail trade was negotiated there, twice as much as in Birmingham or Manchester.* There was a fair amount of industrial life in the area, with six firms employing over 150 workers, and, occasionally, one found large-scale shopping arcades. In the main, however, it seemed as if the suburbs had passed on, leaving a few cultural and economic deposits. By the time the project ended, one or two more small commercial enterprises had been added, thus underlining the point about social and economic pulsations from the centre. But the overwhelming feeling was one of an area abandoned by the middle-class and yet a middle-class content to leave its social debris behind in order to revisit and poke about in it. This feeling was underpinned by the way in which traffic routes seemed usually to take precedence over homes, as the transport appetites, suburbs to centre, were greedily assuaged.

The population of the area was 90,000 in 1966, and, by 1981, it could be as low as 50,000. This decantation moves on apace, with a novel arc of municipal estates being established beyond the suburban crescent at places like Speke, Cantrell Farm and Skelmersdale. 90,000 was 13 per cent of the city population. Of these 16,250 were of school age and 12,000 of pre-school age. The study area percentage of pre-school to total population at thirteen per cent was much higher than the city figure of nine and a half per cent and comparable proportions for the age group 5–14 were eighteen per cent and sixteen per cent respectively.

In 1966 there were some 26,500 households in the designated EPA. Over six in every hundred of them – that is, nearly 1,700 – had more than one to five inhabitants to each room, which was almost three times the city figure of two and a half in every hundred households. Only twenty eight in every hundred – that is, as few as 7,400 – had exclusive use of all the normal amenities, whereas the city figure of sixty in a hundred was twice as high. Relatively few homes were owner-occupied, while the local authority had not numerically made the impact one's first

* W. G. Bor, *Liverpool Interim Planning Policy* (Liverpool Corp.), 1965.

impressions suggested. Alternatively, as many as 14,000 of the houses were privately rented and this, in fact, constituted 20 per cent of Liverpool's privately rented homes. Turning to the area's social composition by occupation, the anticipated weighting at the bottom of the scale soon became apparent. The numbers of persons in classes I and II of the General Register Officer Classification of Occupations (professional and intermediate) was as low as four per cent in some wards, compared with a city figure of twelve per cent, three times as much. Conversely, for class IV and V (partly skilled and unskilled) the same wards had figures as high as fifty-three per cent, a half as much again as the city's thirty-seven per cent figure.

To form some kind of perspective, it is instructive to establish the 'model' EPA situation, over against the 'model' situation in a select Liverpool suburb, of the Woolton or Broad Green type. Seven immediate comparisons of averages might be made:

1. 120 out of every 1,000 EPA houses had more than 1–5 inhabitants to each room;
4 out of every 1,000 suburban houses had more than 1–5 inhabitants to each room.

2. 420 out of every 1,000 EPA houses were shared accommodation;
10 out of every 1,000 suburban houses were shared accommodation.

3. 190 out of every 1,000 EPA houses enjoyed normal amenities (hot water, bath and toilet);
900 out of every 1,000 suburban houses enjoyed normal amenities.

4. 150 out of every 1,000 EPA houses were owner-occupied;
500 out of every 1,000 suburban houses were owner-occupied.

5. 600 out of every 1,000 EPA houses were privately rented;
80 out of every 1,000 suburban houses were privately rented.

6. 40 out of every 1,000 EPA inhabitants were in class I or II of General Register Office Classification;
250 out of every 1,000 suburban inhabitants were in class I or II of General Register Office Classification.

7. 540 out of every 1,000 EPA inhabitants were in class IV or V
of General Register Office Classification;
230 out of every 1,000 suburban inhabitants were in class IV or V
of General Register Office Classification.

These comparisons of extremes only confirmed what observation suggested; namely, that, however blurred sociological dis-
tinctions might have become, type of accommodation, standard
of housing and incidence of occupation clustered together and
found a common level.

The social malaise study recently conducted by the Liverpool
City Planning Department was equally revealing.* The city
wards were ranked according to severity of the incidence of a
number of criteria ranging from school data such as children in
care or pupil absenteeism to community indices such as debt,
possession orders, crime and unemployment. On spot checks
taken in 1967 and 1968, the six wards had well over 30 per cent
of all children in care in Liverpool. In 1967 there were over 1,600
possession orders and over 500 debtors from mid-1967 to mid-
1968. A cursory examination of the crude figures for number of
crimes adds to the crushing evidence of community disturbance
of a severe order in the entire downtown ring of Liverpool. As for
exployment, at the time of the 1966 census count, the unemployment rate in the six wards was astonishingly high at 10 per cent,
and, in August 1968, nearly 30 per cent of all men and women
unemployed in Liverpool for 52 weeks or more were in the study
area. By the winter of 1971, unemployment figures had doubled
and more in some wards and stood at over 20 per cent. Through
the social maze of a busy city, statistics and observation join in
earmarking the two sociometric poles; in Woolton or Broad
Green, the secure professional man enjoying the spacious and
well-appointed delights of owner-occupation; in the EPA, the
unskilled worker (often casually employed or unemployed) shift-
ing and restless in the overcrowded, sub-standard confines of
rented property.

* F. J. C. Amos, *Social Malaise in Liverpool*, City Planning Department,
1970. We are indebted to the Planning Department for permission to quote
from this valuable material, and we have been asked to remind readers of the
obvious limitations of this kind of data.

Education in the Liverpool EPA

But the point was not to upbraid the unsuspecting mortgagees of Broad Green for their good fortune and management, but to enquire whether these distinctive milieux affected children's education critically. It was thus important to examine closely the project schools and their catchment areas. It is worth recording the view of Liverpool planning department in 1965 that 76% of Liverpool's primary schools and 45% of her secondary schools fell short of the Department of Education and Science site standards, that 63% of the primary and 30% of the secondary schools had been built before 1920, and that only 14% of schools had their own playing fields.* It is necessary to recall occasionally that EPA schools, from a physical point of view, are but the worst of a bad lot, and not the odd few in need of renovation to complete a glowing picture. It would be frustrating if, because of the limelight shone on the EPAs, the general parlous nature of educational provision was forgotten.

All the project's twelve primary schools were old. Two were in receipt of grant-aid before the 1870 Education Act; all but one were well established before the 1902 Education Act, and the outstanding one the year Edward VII died. Two of the five county schools had started life as voluntary schools, and one of the others had been among the first group of schools erected by the Liverpool School Board. Three had been all-age schools. They were all typically dark, gaunt, storied structures, one or two of them not without a solid Victorian dignity. None had a grassed playing space, and most had inadequate playgrounds. Only one – with a new hall – had any late extensions. Of themselves they were uninviting places, wholesome at best and deteriorating at worst. A weird but salutary point they practically all had in common was their physical inaccessibility. It was difficult for the stranger to make an entrance. One might march, Jericho-like, around and around, trying to pierce the defences, until one found a tiny gate or a corner door that led to a labyrinth of stairs, rooms, corridors and doors. Not one appeared to have a straight-forward foyer opening on to office or reception accommodation, and, in the early days, the project team was frequently lost with-

* Bor, *op. cit.*

out trace amid one or another of these mazes. This kind of planning fault is but a trivial instance of the overall grievous physical
atmosphere of such schools, with their sombre brickwork, dull
interiors, outmoded amenities, unreliable heating systems and the
rash of minor ailments – broken windows, leaks and so on – that
seems to afflict schools of this date and type. To add to this, they
were often located in a frightening context of decay and devas-
tation. One school in particular stood like an isolated foreign
legion fortress, the only building in a desert of demolition.

Once inside the schools the impression changed considerably.
These were all schools numerically small, and, in most cases,
there was an immediate impact of cosiness and, where not cosiness, anchorage. In every one we were received courteously and
hospitably. All insisted on our visiting informally and without
notice. Cooperation was immediately forthcoming from both
headteachers and staff, and assistance was given generously and
willingly. If 'atmosphere' means anything, then most of the
schools had gone some way to conquering the seemingly in-
surmountable physical obstacles facing them. This note was deliberately recorded at the end of the inaugural six months'
reconnaissance period, before the sentiment bred of prolonged
attachment clouded the vision even more, but, drawing on a
broad experience of school visiting, one's personal and early
judgement was favourably inclined towards the teachers.

This is not to be overdrawn. Some of the teachers, either
through training or predilection, seemed to us to be using inap-
propriate approaches and content. Many, perhaps most of them,
disagreed with our analysis of and hypotheses about the situation. But no one could really doubt the sincerity of their educational views, and the devoted manner in which they applied
them. In the circumstances, the professional attitudes of the
teachers was most impressive, and, whatever the grumblings and
bleatings, morale was not noticeably low. The easy talk of slum
schools producing slum teachers was obviously false. There
seemed, it is true, to be one or two teachers who had discovered a
pleasant niche, where good results were not expected, where
parents were not likely to be bothersome and where 'the office'
would not fuss too much. They did not appear to be in any larger

proportion than those who manage a leisurely existence in any walk of life.

There was, of course, some evidence of turn-over. Still, many teachers provide sound service before 'turning over', and reasons such as promotion, domestic commitment and travel are probably as persuasive as sheer despair. The lack of an immediate pool of teachers living in the area has long been a problem; practically all EPA teachers travel a distance to work. Such areas soon gain a reputation for toughness and awkwardness, and it would be wrong to suggest this is undeserved. Alternatively, it might be said more optimistically that they provide a sharp and vital challenge. Several of our teachers had spent their whole careers, practically their whole lifetimes, in EPA schools. One or two would freely admit that they had not 'turned over' early enough. Others tended to wear hearts on sleeves, and draw self-portraits of themselves as lonely fighters continuing the battle without hope or ally, but no one could deny them this mild pleasure. Nor should it be forgotten that turn-over is probably as much a function of head teacher personality as anything else.

For better or for worse, they appeared then as normal staffs, although this, it must be emphasized, is a personal and arbitrary finding. The first point that occurred to us was that the public relations side of EPA teaching has been woefully feeble. Whatever the factual truth of the matter, most of the teachers saw themselves as a forgotten band, a sort of 14th Army, for whom no one, not HMIs, education committee-men nor LEA officials, cared. EPA folk-lore used to argue that downtown teachers didn't get promotion. Assuredly the entree into the schools was initially not in terms of what the project brought, but purely in that there was recognition that a problem existed. And, apart from the fine challenge of EPA teaching, there are other opportunities. Several of our schools, for instance, planned to accommodate hundreds more than now, given depopulation, they can enroll, offer a treasury of space to the imaginative teacher. Art rooms, animal rooms, television rooms – all these and more are possible in some of the schools, whereas some of the new carefully measured glass structures in the outer suburban ring are very cramped indeed. Including the dozen heads, there were also the equivalent (including part-timers) of 87.7 full-time staff. This gave a pupil–teacher class ratio of 24.1, a most encouraging statistic, especially when set against the city average of 28.1. Some harder facts on these schools may help fill out the picture. Measures of attendance are notoriously unsophisticated guides, but, in the school year 1968/1969, taking the total number of absences as a percentage of the total number of possible attendances, the average for all schools was not unduly large at 13.3 per cent. Length of stay of staff was varied. In one junior mixed and infant school the median length of stay of staff was only five terms, but at the other end of the spectrum one junior department the median length of stay was no less than 17 years. The average length of stay for all project schools was five years one term.*

Pre-school provision was not high in the area, despite its having half the city's nursery schools. An early survey (January 1969) showed that, apart from the three nursery schools, there were seven nursery classes attached to primary schools, seven day nurseries and a dozen or so registered playgroups, child-minders and private nurseries in or near the study area. Allowing for children below the age of three and for children living outside the area, it was estimated approximately that 1,000 children between the ages of three and five were in receipt of any kind of registered pre-school provision. Set against the rough estimate of 6,500 children of nursery age in the area, this implied a grave short-fall. There seemed to be an inverse proportion of need and provision, as compared with some middle-class environs with a large number of privately organized playgroups.

The school's reactions to parents were very varied. None ran an official parent-teacher association, but the schools ran the whole gamut of social gatherings, parental meetings, open days, entertainments, fund-raising activities and informal contacts. Some schools seemed to encourage parents collectively to become involved; others appeared to regard them much more individually and possibly remotely. There was obviously some patronage, and no little outspoken and angry criticism of parents. Several schools obviously felt that they had strong

* Liverpool Education Committee, *Analysis of Primary Schools*, September 1968.

informal links with parents. Despite this variety, there was one constant, and that was the intimate knowledge of family background gleaned by staffs and especially by head teachers. Granted a none too fluent communion between home and school, the very evident grasp by teachers of individual home conditions was extremely noteworthy. This is not to argue that, in each case, the information was utilized sympathetically or beneficially, but its existence was remarkable. Here a comment must be made about the educational welfare officers and the welfare assistants who, the teachers commonly agree, do much to keep the social wheels of the schools smoothly turning. It was this intelligence which made such disturbing reading of the pro formas heads had to complete to apply for EPA status. To take one example, an infant school with about 150 on its registers had an average forty-five pupils leaving each year of whom thirty-nine were moving within the area. Twenty-five were poor attenders or truants, fifty-nine were in need of remedial treatment and sixty-six came from families with four or more children. Only two parents fell into the first four Registrar-General grades of occupational classification, leaving ninety-five as unskilled workers. Fifty-four families were on national assistance, twenty-three children received clothing allowances and twenty-eight had free meals. Most lived in shared and/or unsatisfactory conditions; and thirty-nine were from incomplete families due either to broken marriage or the death of a parent. It added up to a doleful tale of rootless and miserable existence for very many children.

Most of the seven schools had similar records. Poor attendance, large families, unskilled occupations, special difficulties and inadequate housing conditions were frequently and predictably to be found. What was a little surprising was the movement of children, either through rehousing or through what one head called 'disappearing' and another 'flits' on the questionnaire. At one junior school, out of a particular batch only thirty-five spent their four junior years in the school, whereas forty-six others who started in the school were spirited away, in two cases to return to the school at a later date. Another dismal surprise was the sheer quantity of fragmented families. At one school, of a roll of 242, fifty-two pupils were the victims of broken marriage, eleven had a parent dead and twelve lived with either foster-parents or grandparents. At another school with a register of 207, there were twenty-eight broken marriages, nine with one parent dead, twenty-seven unmarried mothers, and ten fostered or with grandparents. A third school had thirty-two with a parent dead. Here the roll was 220. In these cases between a quarter and a third of the school did not experience a normal family setting.*

These head teachers' findings convinced us that the deprivation of the children we were dealing with during the project was unhappily extensive and that, in the phrases of the DES circular 11/67, which had been concerned with the problem of defining deprivation for the £75 award, there was considerable 'multiple deprivation', and the 'general quality of physical existence' was poor. Naturally enough, the teachers in the schools well-versed in the data of the children's 'physical existence' eked out the skeletal bones of the findings with tragic case-histories. There were some incidents of ill-treatment and several of neglect. There was a woman, alone and reduced through illness to five and a half stone, trying to cope with a young family in a seventh storey flat. During an early walk through the area, one witnessed a pregnant woman chasing her two small sons from their dilapidated shell, which was without doors or windows and with most of the roof missing, hitting one with a wildly flung screwdriver and cursing angrily the while. The anecdotal accounts of life in the area were colourful and vivid. Alongside the many orthodox existences, there seemed to be several that were to say the least unconventional, with children living in the very shadow of crime and vice. Not all these existences were by any means unhealthy. This portends to be descriptive rather than critical. The essential issue was to accept that, in a deprived area, children often live in a social context widely at variance with normal experience. For many EPA children it is insufficient to think of 'ordinary' everyday life pitched in a lower register. One must conceive of a difference in kind rather than degree.

Yet given the theme of deprivation, the variations upon it are manifold. This was readily seen in the schools. There was no flat, common EPA problem. It was disconcerting as well as stimu-

* Liverpool Education Committee, *Assessment of EPA Schools*, Sc/212/10(a), 1968.

lating to observe the variety even among these schools. A large part of the variation was because of the personal commitment of head teachers, who, as ever, stamped their character and viewpoint on each school. One school might see reading to be the key, and drive formally and strenuously to that end. Another might feel that social training was the leading answer, and place its emphasis there. Another might attempt to draw liberally on the attitudes and substance of the suburban school, in order to compensate for inadequate environment. Another might seek constantly to seize on novel ways to engage the purported short-term interest of its EPA pupils. Another might turn more readily to the guide-line and security of religion and the family. Another might hope to relax and release the children through a widening scope of creative experience. Another might choose to construct a haven for the pupils, happily but firmly organized.

On the other hand, the problem varied. Against the bleak canvas of multi-deprivation, one or other factor seemed, for each school, to be outstanding. Here it was the immigrant issue and the attendant language difficulty. There it was the social and mental problems associated with highrise residence, and many teachers near to this situation believed that the EPA problem actually began with the replacement of terraced housing by blocks of flats. Here it was primarily a staffing or structural difficulty. There it was the problem of social mobility and declining numbers. The common denominator was that of teachers attempting, by their own lights, to raise the educational performance of the children, but everywhere grappling with huge social obstacles.

All the children in the study schools and three other central EPA schools were tested near the commencement of the exercise as part of the baseline evaluation. At this point the single necessary point may briefly be made. The 2,574 children who were tested in the project schools and three control schools on the English Picture Vocabulary Test of listening comprehension scored an average well below the national average standardized score of 100. The range was from 84.9 in one junior department to 96.6 in a nursery school. Most schools fell in the 85 to 95 range. This compared with a mean standardized score of 111.4 from ten classes in a suburban school and located in a largely middle-class area. This, of course, was entirely predictable in terms of all we have learned over the last decades about the relationship of social disadvantage and educational attainment. The late Professor Wiseman's survey in the Plowden Report argued convincingly that 'home' and 'neighbourhood' variables amounted to a very heavy loading as against 'school' variables when correlated with educational attainment.* J. W. B. Douglas demonstrated how lower working-class children in unsatisfactory accommodation, especially in large families with little parental interest shown, fared very badly as against their upper middle-class peers in satisfactory and encouraging situations.† It is just impossible to doubt the effect of detrimental conditions on a child's education. Whereas sixteen of a normal suburban class of thirty might expect to move on to grammar school or the top stream equivalent in a comprehensive school, perhaps only four of an EPA class of thirty would usually achieve this success. As for higher education, while maybe four or five of the suburban group might enjoy the privilege, the law of averages would really have to be favourably inclined for two of the EPA group so to succeed. Children born and living in a badly disadvantaged district assuredly have the educational dice loaded against them.

The EPA – a dislocated community

And the Liverpool EPA community certainly was a dislocated and transitional one, with its incidence of social malaise, by the normally received standards, high. There was vandalism and petty theft, some of it spreading downwards into the primary schools. On the other hand, there were several vigorously thriving community associations and neighbourhood groups, with councillors, social workers and volunteers and local residents extremely active. In community centres and at street meetings there was a veritable buzz of involvement. There was a proliferation of social workers, employed both by public and by voluntary agencies. One's first guess was that such a haphazard network of welfare attempts must dissipate energy alarmingly. Area community wardens, probation officers, community service volun-

* S. Wiseman, 'The Manchester Survey', App. IX, *Plowden Report*, ii, (1967).

† J. W. B. Douglas, *Home and School* (1964).

teers, juvenile liaison officers, various charitable societies, child care officers, health visitors, an extensive 'Shelter' project – these and many others joined the myriad ranks of those bringing much needed help to the area. Generally speaking, this array of social workers was full of sympathy, huge effort and progressive ideas.

The professional and social structure within which they worked underlined the lack of communal identity. It seemed, once we began work inside the deprived area, that threads crept out from Whitehall and from town hall, each hoping to meet a separate need, be it in education, housing, health or whatever. By the time these threads reached the area, they were strained to snapping point and often entangled in a frustrating knot. For this reason proposals to rationalize local government within large-scale regional units had their less attractive aspects. Efforts to rouse the local citizenry to participate politically were sometimes rewarding, especially when the aims – the provision of washing facilities or the maintenance of drains – were highly relevant and short-term. The foci for these endeavours were very localized and always changing. There was no constant 'downtown' point of identity for political anchor. This meant, at all times, that the designated EPA was never more than an artefact, and this lack of obvious structural or political entity was ever a stumbling-block both to research and, arguably, to the improvement of the area.

What were the initial general impressions of the EPA? These were, of course, fleeting and ill formed, the visual bric-à-brac gathered by pounding the beat through the area. They included a strong impression of the variety of the area, from the little old terraced homes, often impeccably trim, to the soaring towers of flats, frequently as distinctly ill-kempt and tarnished. There seemed to be acres of rubble everywhere, with weeds and dumped rubbish beginning to materialize on top of the razed masonry and charred woodwork. The stench of the fires lit by demolition gangs was the characteristic odour, with the usual cases of residents hanging grimly on, as neighbouring homes burnt and toppled around them. At this close view the sweeping amputations of the planners seemed raw and crude, with the knife used as unswervingly as Dr Cutler's in 'The Doctor's Dilemma'.

Sometimes it was a strong, solid building that was destined for destruction; again, one might suddenly arrive upon a pleasing terraced crescent that was due to die.

One quickly learned that emotions were just as significant as rational thoughts when it came to social issues like planning. There were homes that were being destroyed, and, with them, perhaps lengthy filial and group traditions. Probably some of the anti-authoritarian tendencies of the area were, predictably enough, motivated by the upset and turmoil of life in Liverpool 7 and Liverpool 8. But, infinitely sadder than any vandalism or small-scale crime, was the resignation of those who found themselves unable to cope. Ground down by the ceaseless difficulties facing them, they had no longer even boot-straps by which to haul themselves up. No glib half-truths about laziness or working harder sprang to mind; rather was it a case of there but for the grace of God.

At the same time the study area was full of vitality and rich in character. The cosmopolitan mix of Liverpool has bred splendid resources of popular culture. At a top level it has created an almost North American tradition of what F. J. Turner called 'vital entertainers'. It is locally to be observed in the many pubs and corner shops. Collectively, it may be witnessed on Liverpool's Spion Kop or Everton's Gwladys Street each Saturday. It may be seen in the astounding spectacle of an Orange Day parade in Southport or in the processions of witness in the many Roman Catholic churches. Whether it be the World Cup at Goodison Park or the opening of the Metropolitan Cathedral, flats and streets are ornately decorated as if by magic. The Liverpudlian is as much a wall-dauber as the Sorbonne student. Alongside the whitewashed theological slogans, in support of a Heenan or a Paisley, the saints of the modern dispensation, like Joe Royle or Tommy Smith, are celebrated. There is point and counter-point. To 'God Bless Our Pope', the Protestant Loyalist can scarce forbear to add 'ye'. Possibly the character of the EPA is epitomized by the precisely painted goalposts on the wall of a block of flats, directly under a notice forbidding children from playing football in the precinct.

The overall social problem is an awesome one, but perhaps the surprise is that it is not more so. Given the appalling social conditions, the spirit and response of the large majority of the residents, and the teachers and other professionals who serve them, is remarkably valiant and encouraging. Above all, the cheerful resilience and unquenchable courage of the children in the face of the most debilitating and distressing circumstances is little short of miraculous. To recall the starting point of the survey, two hundred years' social history had dealt these children a crippling hand. Was it possible to alter this deep-rooted situation?

3 The Method
The Technique of Action Research

Action and research: A confrontation

Ours was called an action-research programme and this was the cue for immediate conflict between actionists and researchers as to which work should be uppermost. There were men of action who resented what they regarded as the cloying, inhibiting attentions of pristine researchers. There were men of research who were driven neurotic by the wild abandon of actionists whose ventures they found difficult to circumscribe long enough to measure. Each project was established in conjunction with the appropriate local authority and university, with an obvious bias towards action and research respectively. The Liverpool project was particularly fortunate to enjoy the sagacious counsels of the LEA Chief Inspector, Tom McManners, together with the astute discernment of Professor Alan Blyth of Liverpool University's Institute of Education, and, at this personal level, the structure worked very happily.

Nonetheless, nationally and conceptually, there was some chance of a project not unlike Dr Doolittle's Pushmepullyou, of which, in the musical film version of that zoologist's adventures, Richard Attenborough claimed that 'I've never seen anything like it in my life'. On the one hand, a senior education official was heard to remark that experimental research was 'infamous' and that, vis-à-vis EPAs, the only research necessary was 'to look out of the bloody window'. On the other hand, a university lecturer plaintively remarked that 'no one would take any notice of the project's work unless it was based upon experimental research'; which seemed like saying that only people with dirty minds would read pornography. There could have been, then, a clash of functions, with LEAs and project directors working hard to alleviate obvious educational distress and universities and research officers concentrating on precise measurement of tested results.

There was an early instance of this difficulty in the Liverpool project. It could not have been earlier. It occurred on the first day, 1 October 1968. I met the heads of the twelve project schools for luncheon and, immediately, it was obvious that research was a hot potato. Apart from the teachers' professional suspicion of educational research, there was, in this case, a particular feature. J. B. Mays, Professor of Social Sciences at Liverpool University, had published a book in 1962 called *Education and the Urban School,* which was based upon his researches in what was now called the Educational Priority Area. Whatever the actual merits of this work might be, there is no doubt it was greeted with bitter resentment by the local teaching force. I had heard some wind of this previously, but I had not quite reckoned for its gale force implications. At this first heads' lunch, I learned in no uncertain manner that, apropos research, I had better tread carefully.

If a research was a hot potato, then it was worth recalling Samuel Johnson's remark, when, after spitting out a piece of potato that burned him in the presence of the king: 'a fool, sire,' said Johnson, 'would have kept it in.' Research had, temporarily at least, to be spat out, and it was several weeks before Keith Pulham, the project's research officer, deemed it wise to move into the schools. Matters were not helped by Professor Mays' presence on our local steering committee; in the event, he attended only the first two meetings, and, on 1 May 1969, he wrote an article in the *Guardian* entitled 'the Research Smokescreen', which attacked the basic structure of the project. We had this photocopied and distributed to all project schools and this cleared the air considerably, in that staffs were able to note the element of disagreement between the professor and ourselves.

Nationally, a compromise was agreed. There was a decision to promote two pieces of pure research nationally; one, the collation of baseline data from all project areas, aiming at an intense profile of the EPA situation; two, a pre-school language experiment. Beyond that, there was an agreement to grant a substantial amount of autonomy to local action teams to pursue what action – within the most general terms of community schooling – they found fitting and to describe their work in as careful a manner as possible. This, in turn, avoided another possible cleavage – that between a national pattern and parochial endeavours locally. As it was, a de facto division of labour manifest itself on the projects, with different areas opting for different emphases, given different situations and the different predelictions of the project teams.

It was odd attending national conferences. What seemed a monstrous intrusion on a school's time and format appeared to be but a slight and minuscule dent against a national canvas. When in Liverpool, one felt highly Liverpool-oriented; at national conference level, one, predictably, appreciated the weight of a national undertaking. On the whole, the locality orientation remained uppermost, partly because officers had been appointed *before* a plan of campaign had been drawn and thus they naturally gravitated to their native heaths and partly because – once it was accepted that community schooling was the prior theme – it automatically followed that there would be important differences. It is the essence of the Community School that it is tailored to the texture of the particular community, and, therefore, a choice of five widely varying districts was a sound idea.

It was also important that the local education authorities were engaged substantially. Apart from the absolutely indispensable nature of their assistance and entrée, it was to stand us in good stead when the projects ended. Many such ventures have in the past been all too clearly described in the words of the hymn sung in several schools where they have taken place: they have blossomed and flourished like leaves on a tree, then withered and perished. So many projects have been born amidst scenes of wild enthusiasm only to die alone and unmourned. Of a recent well-publicized and largescale curriculum project, its progenitor recently replied, when asked where examples could be observed, that there was one in New Brunswick and one in Ontario. The EPA Project Directors, fairly hardened and veteran campaigners, were always forewarned of this type of calamity and worked strenuously to ensure that much of their work would continue after the project period ended. But the other crucial factor was the commitment of the LEAs. I think it fair to state that the continuity of work in the EPA project districts is well above the norm for such programmes, and it has been the engagement of the local authorities and their natural wish to sustain their own investments which has proved critical. Whereas other projects, funded by the charitable foundations or the Schools Council, have often worked more directly with schools, the local authorities were intimately concerned with the funding and operation of the EPA Projects, and they are the agencies capable of maintaining action. It is worth noting for future negotiation that the wholehearted involvement, financial and administrative, of a local authority is, as well as its many other advantages, some guarantee of sustenance.

Certainly the Liverpool local education authority, at officer and member level, proved a hospitable and encouraging host to the project, and, insofar as it was a success, the project owed much to the cooperation and support proffered by the LEA. One is less certain of the role of the universities in the context of social intervention programmes. At an Anglo-American Conference in 1970 on the subject of such programmes, Marty Rein, now of the Massachusetts Institute of Technology, described what he called 'the seven plagues of Egypt'. These were the calamities that had befallen social intervention schemes in the United States. Top of his list of epidemica was using universities for research. It is a wry thought that, because of the unrivalled grasp of social evaluation, the agility of analysis of social problems and the determined commitment and leadership of A. H. Halsey, National Director of the EPA Projects, the purportedly creaking medieval institution of Oxford University where Dr Halsey is head of Social and Administrative Studies, seems better placed than any other British university to assist in social reform.

Compared with the help proffered by the LEA university support was not so very extensive, except for the welcome and much valued support of Professor Alan Blyth. We had a series of unlucky ventures with the university. For instance, the Architecture department offered, for £150 expenses, to plan and model an EPA Community School to our remit. This was an exciting enterprise, which could have set off our final report vividly. It was promised for 1 December 1970. A brief document and £65 change apart, we're still waiting. In 1971 the students proposed to hold an arts festival and persuaded us to involve some twenty

EPA schools. Partway through the preparations, with money spent, children stimulated and teachers engaged, the festival was abandoned without warning or discussion. After considerable lobbying, the Students Union did fork out some funds to cover the expense, but, to retain the good will of our client schools and to avoid disappointing dozens of children, we had to organize our own festival. At short notice and at a time when pressures made such an activity difficult, we mounted 'Cityscenes' (a rather clumsy play on 'citizens'), an exhibition both live and static, of schoolwork based on the environment. Titles like 'the Great Fire of Liverpool', 'the Everton Sound', 'Looking at Liverpool', 'Liverpool Through the Seasons' and 'the Folk who live in Our Street' illustrate the richness of the vein, and it was a shame that such imaginative work did not receive its due publicity.

It is the unreliability of university commitment which makes one, in practice, most chary of inviting their assistance. Whether the more leisurely pace of academic life, with its pleasing vacations and ivoried towers, is to blame, one can't be sure. Certainly the tempo of the university seems to be completely out of harmony with the urgent, busy, contractual nature of socially committed projects. It is as if they cannot be trusted except absolutely on their own terms.

But it is the university as a negation of action that is the most bothersome feature, and here one thinks not particularly of Liverpool, although it has its staunch representatives of the genre, nor, of course, of all university teachers, although probably no college lacks its delegates to the grand conference of academic inaction. This is not a general anti-research complaint, it is a criticism of that touching, clutching faith in a purportedly pristine 'objectivity' that threatens to bring any attempt to change things grinding to a halt. It borders on the anal-erotic. It wants to stop life in order to measure static, that is, unreal, situations, and, in its efforts to avoid 'contamination' and a too generous bounty of 'variables', it so limits and cabins and confines that little effective is ever realized. It is fearful of dirtying its hands on anything that cannot be rigorously tubbed whiter-than-white in the acadamic lanolin of the research washer.

In a word, it lacks guts. It is frightened of subjectivity, although subjectivity has much to offer if you don't pretend it's objectivity. As such, it appears to exclude so much of life and experience. Don't university psychologists fall in love? This lack of fire and this unwillingness to risk an occasional boob in the face of obvious social injustice is best illustrated by the persistent wail that 'we don't *really* know how children are deprived so how can we help them?' God knows that it is true, but we can't idle away years, doing nothing about self-evident, glaring situations, while the purists distil their fine essence until, doubtless, it is unadulterated enough for publication and too unadulterated for use.

Several universities are stuck right in the middle of deprived areas, are, in fact, EPA landlords and are responsible indeed for some of the developments which contribute to the havoc of inner city replanning; this only adds to the irony. There are just too few examples of gown helping downtown, even of sharing facilities with the community despite the long vacations and so on. There is too seldom a helping hand; there is scarcely ever – certainly at an institutional level – a positive lead to ameliorate the condition and circumstances of the university's neighbours. A year or so back, the Liverpool University students sat in at the Senate House (until the attraction of the Easter Holiday proved too compelling) in righteous protest against some policy of the university. Did it never occur to them to make their probably well-merited strike a positive rather than a negative action by a vast piece of community service in the slums or on the demolition sites not a hundred yards from where they were? There are good omens – the Student Community Action movement organized by Ray Phillips is one, but not many and the universities have an impoverished record in terms of Educational Priority Areas.

Action research: A third discipline

The research dilemma was even more troublesome in Liverpool where we decided to mount what was, in a sense, a philosophical inquiry, and not simply an investigation of educational psychology and sociology. It has been said that psychology and sociology have, over the last twenty years, performed an excellent service of highlighting special problems such as social deprivation, but that it is now the turn of the educational philosopher to come up with some directives. Hence our project was a 'philosophic practice' one. It was to be an inquiry searching for questions rather than answers, and this made the research prospects fearful and discouraging. In action-research, there are enough difficulties in any event. As Michael Young wrote, 'You can easily have innovation without research – the fashions which periodically sweep through the educational world are witness to that. You can, and almost always do, have research without innovation.'* Coupling the two is many times more difficult than attempting either apart, but a few comments from the action side might be helpful at this stage.

Firstly, it soon became apparent that no once-for-all separation of function was practicable, and that the Research Officer was to be a man of action just as the Project Director had to perform research duties. This stemmed from the simple conclusion that action-research was not the conjunction of two operations, but a discipline best seen as an entity in itself with its own regulo and justification. Any attempt to match the organic and subjective commitment of sheer action with the inorganic and objective concern of pure research was doomed to be a futile one.

Secondly, this entailed a close working partnership, with practically a day to day examination of function, that duplication and waste of effort might to some degree be avoided. Once decided on a framework or principle of action, the innovation and evaluation became frequently inseparable, as each influenced the style of the other and the team strove to balance the dispassionate and the committed parts of its make-up. Action-research for us, differed from research alone chiefly in its avoidance of the static, controlled and contrived model and its emphasis on a fluent, ongoing approach, one not afraid to attempt properly guarded assessments in unpropitious circumstances. Action-research differed from action alone mainly in the constant feeding back of evaluation and the effect this had on crucial shifts of direction in the action.

Thirdly, interpretative description, rather than the bright eulogy of action or the sadfaced tabulations of research, was the attempted medium for relating the results of the project. It is stressed that this is not often academic method research; on the

* M. Young, *Innovation and Research in Education*, Routledge and Kegan Paul, 1969.

other hand, it would be as hotly disputed that it is, within its own terms, academic. There is ample precedent in scholarship for factual collation and personal opinion going hand in hand, and this, however grievous the results, was the basis of our work. We would paraphrase E. H. Carr's point about the continuous process of interaction and the unending dialogue between facts and their interpreters.* An illustration of this was the, for us, discovery that action-research needs to be underway before the process of interaction begins. Three weeks of doing something was immeasurably more valuable in terms of what we should be doing than three months wondering and debating what to do.

So much for research. After the action dilemma and the problem of research, a third query, that of audience had to be raised. Towards whom was the project directed? There was a possible select university audience, but one felt that this might not take too kindly to the empiricism of our action research and that, in any case, it was not positioned to implement large scale reforms as a consequence of any recommendations. At the opposite end of the scale, an EPA project was hardly likely to provide the stuff of a rattling yarn for the general reader. This left the educational practitioners; the inspectorate, the committee-men, governors and managers, LEA officials and advisers, and the teachers themselves. Only among this group might one expect to engage a ready sympathy for our attitude, and, more meaningfully, these were the ones most able to put in train possible recommendations.

Inquiry among this fraternity showed signs that this was not too idle an assessment. Most of those with whom we discussed the matter were interested in what HMIs call 'good practice'. It was argued that research results did not necessarily persuade, and that educational change progressed rather by precepts culled from in-service courses, teacher centres, inspectoral advice and so on. Like the legendary drunkard with the lamp-post, statistics were useful for support not for illumination. We were visibly shaken by the suspicion and hostile reaction of many teachers in the study area to the very mention of research. Certainly priority areas had become a trifle fashionable, and teachers found it galling to be subject to the kind of academic voyeurism that watched, noted and departed. Visible practice seemed the soundest possi-

* E. H. Carr, *What is History?*, Penguin, 1964.

bility. Accordingly, we decided that action-research must not only be done, but must be seen to be done.

One conceived then, not of a possible audience of research readers, but of an audience of action observers. These could be likened to a gunnery target. The bull's eye was the children, teachers and parents in the project schools. If they did not feel somehow the better for the project, then most was lost. The inner band of the target was a spatial momentum in terms of spreading what benefits might accrue from the project to Liverpool's other EPA schools. The magpie ring was a temporal momentum, a determination that the project would establish agencies and communications that might ensure some continuance of these benefits when the project ended. The outer ring was the rest of Merseyside and those authorities and teachers on its fringes who might be interested in the project. The team was encouraged to think so grandiosely by the several indications of such interest during the opening weeks of the exercise.

In retrospect, one might possibly argue that it was unwise to appoint separate action and research officers, or, at least, we should now seek out ways of training action-researchers in a third and separate sphere. Keith Pulham, the Liverpool research officer, had had experience of empirical public research with the civil service, and this proved invaluable in the somewhat heated tempo of action-research. A durable, cheerful and loyal colleague, he wholeheartedly committed hmself to the need to balance action and research. 'Interpretation' was widely used, therefore, in lieu of either 'evaluation', with its exacting, inhibiting overtones, or the random activity of goalless practice. Like lunacy and sanity, a thin line separates the union of action-research from the halfcock confusion of a slab of action and a slab of research. We attempted to muster our regulo, refusing to accept the blandishments of the all-out actionists or the austere strictures of the extremist researcher. Naturally enough, we often failed to negotiate a flawless route between the cavaliers of 'good practice' and the roundheads at prayer in their devotional research chapels.

'Interpretation' meant assembling what evidence was available, submitting it flexibly to the theoretical frame of community education, and making decisions accordingly. It accepted that time and evidence were sometimes in short supply, but viewed this as a factor for consideration rather than a reason for postponement of action. It refused to ignore the possible value of subjective judgement; indeed, personal assessments on what data could be assembled was the major tactic. One soon grew tired of gurus making holy and noble noises about their 'objectivity', when all manner of subjective motivations – need to impress similarly disposed academic colleagues, anxiety about promotion – were so patently apparent.

If anything, the Liverpool project erred on the side of overmuch action and too little research. This lay perhaps in the nature of the exercise and the audience for whom it was intended. Luckily, Keith Pulham was eminently suited for the kind of social survey much of the research entailed. It was often even arithmetic. For instance, a home-school activity was not investigated primarily for its effect on the education of the children, but for its capacity to attract the parents. Similarly, our preschool action was chiefly about the quantity rather than the quality of provision for EPA under-fives. We tried to get the horse before the cart. This is not to deny the need to examine the effect of parental engagement or the content of pre-school programmes, but, as a matter of priority, we need to know how to obtain the commitment of parents and provide pre-school places before there is much point or, in fact, possibility of experimenting with effects.

The matching of 'real' and 'ideal'

If 'interpretation' was the technique employed to assess action, how were the sinews of action themselves laid bare? We erected an 'ideal' – that of the urban Community School – but there was little point in calmly delineating for a school the golden dawn that was their birthright and expecting it to be made manifest by 9.00 a.m. the following morning. Over against the ideal, was the 'real', the taut circumstances in which the EPA schools were operating. This was emphasized amusingly for us in the early weeks of the project by a glorious paradox related by a teacher who was not anxious to entertain project activities. Now every town has its 'Baker Avenue' school, that suburban idyll, that sceptred isle set in a gilded sea, the envy of those teachers who rejoice in the quiescent and quiveringly bright responses of well-scrubbed uppermiddleclass juniors. This teacher told us how dreadful his school was and he recited all the Plowden criteria of deprivation to justify his opinion. It was so uptight that even help would dislocate. 'If you want to do a project like this,' he cried, 'why don't you do it at Baker Avenue?' So we had to join in dialogue with the schools, trying to match their pace and encourage them to march a trifle quicker, often assisting them to adopt tactics they might have themselves attempted had finance and time and energy allowed. Our only proviso was that each step taken was in the direction of the Community School.

By these means we endeavoured to relate real and ideal, or, to put it another way, theory and practice. A hypothetical frame of reference was planned and, inevitably, the theory was necessarily adjusted at the dictates of practice, just as the practice was submitted to the strictures of theory. I once heard A. H. Halsey tell an American asking for reading on the principles of action-research to study volume I of E. H. Carr's *The Bolshevik Revolution*. It was not a piece of scholarly one-upmanship. Whatever one's feelings about his politics, there can be no brooking the argument that Lenin is the most successful project director to emerge this century, and, as E. H. Carr makes clear, it is this harmonious balancing of theory and practice upon which his triumph was most securely based. 'It was this union of theory and practice which made Lenin,' wrote Carr, 'a complex figure and accounted for his unique greatness. . . . In the roll of Lenin's genius one of the largest entries would have to be devoted to his greatness as a political strategist and as a political tactician. . . . His farsightedness in building up impregnable positions in advance was matched by an uncanny instinct which told him where to and when and how to strike or to hold back.' Or, as Lenin himself wrote, 'it is not enough to be a revolutionary and an advocate of socialism in general. It is necessary to know at every moment, how to find the particular link in the chain which must be grasped with all one's strength in order to keep the whole chain in place and prepare to move on resolutely to the next link.'*

It is a far cry from the epic proportions of the 1917 Russian Revolution to two or three lads pattering around the backstreets

* E. H. Carr, *The Bolshevik Revolution*, vol. 1, pp. 35–6 (Penguin edition), 1950.

of Liverpool. Nor would one dream of attempting to emulate perhaps the master action-research officer of all time. But this gelling of theory and practice was an all-important cue. Without a vision, the 'sun' of the Community School, we could have easily found ourselves floundering with ad hoc pick-me-ups and bits and pieces of superficial amelioration. Without a sensitivity for the stern reality of the EPA situation, we could as easily have found ourselves vainly peddling a false or distant hope, with the school drawbridges up before we had scarcely begun. The harmony of ideal and real further necessitated a flexible approach, what Lenin might himself have called a 'dialectical' and not a dogmatic approach. Practice might alter in terms of changed circumstance or in recognition of theoretical shifts; theory might change in response to fresh argument or, more likely, fresh data suggesting new directions. But the one, ideally, should never be out of flunker with the other. Practice should never stifle theory; theory should never confine practice.

Disraeli, a notorious dunce at geography, was once asked where the Virgin Isles were. 'I do not know, ma'am,' he replied, 'but I am sure they are as far as possible from the Isle of Man.' Sometimes the chasm between action and research or between practice and theory appeared as wide. But to close the gap was our steadfast hope, and it is now, with some trepidation, our mild boast, that this pair of dichotomies was drawn together into a double marriage, happy enough to raise even Disraeli's cynical eyebrow.

4 The Approach
Building a Team and a Programme

Recruitment and reconnaissance

It was initially important to establish a network of command, liaison and communication. Working in an Educational Priority Area involves an awfully large moral obligation. One is rightly anxious not to scatter resources and beat up enthusiasm before departing and leaving everyone bereft. This is deplorable enough anywhere, but, in a socially disadvantaged situation, this was of a more compelling consideration. Thus one tended to take some care with the construction of a nexus of communications, hopeful that it would remain hardy enough to sustain some perpetuation of the action. It is not without relish that we can record that each of the major administrative structures we created is still in business and, if anything, expanding.

The local education authority invited a number of interested persons to act as a Local Steering Committee, and this was composed of some dozen education officials, others working in education and one or two private individuals. We were fortunate in our education committee members, for the two chairmen of the Steering Committee – first Councillor N. A. Pannell and then Alderman C. Dickenson – were also at the same time Chairman of the Liverpool Education Committee. It was of much value that such influential members felt strongly enough to give so generously of their time and energy, while a second education committee member – Councillor Mrs Margaret Simey – offered the Steering Committee her characteristic zeal and crispness of analysis throughout the entire project period. These beneficial links with the higher echelons of Liverpool's educational management underline an earlier point about the value of relating LEAs with activities like ours, and, needless to say, when it came to talk on continuing the project action, these were staunch allies indeed. The Steering Committee gave unstintingly of advice and encouragement, but, like all the best of its kind, most of its members worked hard for the project in their specialist capacities away from the actual meetings. One always felt that friends were operating skilfully on one's behalf. One member went so far, half-jokingly, as to say that the least important thing the Steering Committee did was to meet!

The project team was initially composed of Marie Byrne, Secretary to the Project, Keith Pulham, the Action-research Officer and myself as Director. Luckily, Keith Pulham fell in eagerly with the philosophy and with the method enunciated, and, as well as undertaking the research programme dictated by national needs, he introduced several important action initiatives and supported the whole action schedule in general. One was as likely to find him humping rabbit food into a school's animal room as poring over his computerized mysteries or lecturing on pre-school language structures. The two officers, with Marie Byrne as pleasingly friendly and competent secretary, were financed out of project funds, and it was but one of the oddities of the situation that, for three years, I was, technically, paid as a Reader of Oxford University.

As well as assembling a network of professional communication around this team, occasion arose for and necessity demanded an augmentation of the fulltime staff. For instance, Trilby Shaw, a sparkling and popular worker, was employed as an Assistant Action-research Officer for some eighteen months of the project. During the first year of our work, however, two other developments occurred. First, David Connor, the district secretary of the Workers' Educational Association, proposed that a WEA tutor-organizer should be attached to the project to examine adult education in the context of the EPA idea. In September 1969 Tom Lovett arrived from battle-scarred Belfast to commence what turned out to be a most fruitful and challenging experiment in adult education. Second, and at much the same time, John Moores Junior (a member of our Local Steering Committee) and his wife, Jane underlined their keen interest in the pre-school aspect of education for the socially disadvantaged by establishing a Pre-school Fellowship funded by the Moores Family Charity Foundation. This interesting precedent – business backing for work among the under fives in the backstreets of Liverpool – was, of course, most heartening. Eleanor Connor was appointed the Moores Pre-school Fellow, and she began the pioneer task of strengthening the quality of community pre-school provision in a way which has caused considerable comment and admiration. These two new colleagues added fore and aft dimensions to the school-centred exploits of the project. If not exactly ensuring a cradle to grave range of action, Eleanor Connor interposed between cradle and school, just as Tom Lovett filled some of the gap between school and grave. It is worth noting now that, in terms of continuity, both these officers remain in their jobs in the post-project dispensation, and the team has been increased still further. We were also fortunate in building up a small, devoted band of voluntary helpers, who assisted in distribution of publications and so on. Beyond that, we retained two people for specialist functions, paying them what, in terms of their contribution, was no more than a monthly pittance. Terry Mulrooney was our Mr Fixit, the agent for many of our purchases, an untiring noser-out of the finest bargains and an acknowledged expert in the provision of often eccentric-sounding resources. David Appleton was our Art Designer and his striking art-work became a notable feature of our presentations and was one of the secrets of the excellent publicity we normally enjoyed.

The first three to six months was spent in a reconnaissance of the area. This had a triple purpose. First, it enabled the project officers to familiarize themselves with the district, its schools and its problems; second, it gave the area an opportunity to learn about the project and to accustom itself to our presence; third, it was a period of dialogue between the project and the schools and other bodies, during which the major planks of the programme were constructed. In our action-research the issue of dialogue was all-important. It was neither possible nor desirable to contrive situations or to force an unnatural pace. One could move only as fast as the schools wished. This was only fair. By accepted standards, the schools were mainly working as well as, granted the circumstances, one had a right to expect. The head teachers and some of each staff were long experienced in 'downtown' teaching. The organization of a 'downtown' school is frequently a delicately poised affair, because of staffing, building and other difficulties, and it is easily unhinged by irregular or extra impositions. To have wished preconceived notions and programmes on to these schools would, therefore, have been as much naïve as arrogant. Not only that, but we had a question to ask – simply; are the schools relevant? – and not as yet any solution to offer. Any attempt to descend, Christ-like, to cleanse the temple, was to be strictly avoided.

EPA teachers have a very understandable sensitivity. Many of them have seen researchers come and go without a trace; they have watched reports, enthusiastically compiled, gather dust on the shelves; they have heard bland assurances and facile promises, and their whole experience rightly puts them on their guard. Their belief is that, by and large, the suburban schools are better treated in every way. What, briefly, was so special about us that we would divert from the norm? Further, (and granted our sincerity), who were we that we might know more or better than the teachers actually doing the job? There was a suspicion that appointments made under the ivory-towered auspices of Oxford University ('South of the border', as one voice described it) would have little worthwhile to offer Liverpool 7 and 8.

Thus, the reconnaissance proved to be a tricky challenge. The first term was a ceaseless round of appointments, visits and meetings, probably one hundred and fifty in all, with the Research Officer and I sharing the duties in order to complete them. In the second term, when much of the programme was being shaped, we worked together much more often. Schools apart, there was a heavy round of talks to groups and invitations to attend conferences and meetings. The EPA vogue was beginning to swell, and, although we made every effort to fulfil all these requests, there were some where our attendance seemed peripheral and even wholly unnecessary. It was difficult to draw the distinction, as it were, between the useful and the ornamental. Among the most interesting of these agencies were the several luncheon clubs in the area, mainly composed of visiting professionals – teachers, social workers, clergy and the like – who met informally to hear speakers and share problems. Membership overlapped, so that the clubs formed a kind of gastronomic Mafia and both Project Director and Research Officer were soon established on this circuit. We were received kindly and they paid us the compliment of being fiercely contentious; 'is this dangerous philosophy you preach', I was once sternly asked, 'your own or that of your masters at Oxford?' These discussions introduced us to the area, and, just as important, they forced us to clear our heads a little and streamline our thoughts.

The programme: The primary school

As the project was post-Plowden, the primary school aspect was naturally placed at the centre of our programme. From September to Christmas of 1968, negotiations with the schools proceeded. The head teachers were initially lunched together; then each was visited and, eventually, each staff was addressed. A Teachers' Liaison Group was immediately formed, and this met weekly until December. Each school was informally represented on this group, which acted as a go-between for project and staffs and as a sounding board for suggestions. By this device, we were able to float ideas and evoke fairly swift responses. Meetings were not too structured and some schools preferred to change their representation so that more than one teacher might become involved.

One slight change in its composition might, in retrospect, have been helpful. Perhaps it was formed too precipitately. The heads and schools could not have been too clear what was required, and it may have been wiser to have become acquainted more intimately with the staffs before allowing such a group to emerge. Sometimes an appointee seemed rather on the defensive, so that one felt one was not selling the project enthusiastically in that school; if, as occasionally happened, another teacher in the same school became highly interested in the project, the existence of a different representative could be a small obstacle. This is but a tiny point, for, by and large, the Liaison Group was a sound one and needed to start immediately the project began. As for the Standing Committee of Headteachers, which soon settled down to a bi-termly luncheon meeting, this always proved to be a lively and uninhibited body, probably more so than the teachers' committee. The heads were honest enough to offer one reason for this: namely, any kudos arising from the project tended to come their way, while most of the hard graft was done by the classroom teacher. They may have been a trifle modest; it was quite obvious how most of them had been selected as head teachers, for they were a most personable and gifted group, with little or none of that conservatism that is purported to weigh heavily on those set in elevated places. Suffice it to say that, like the Local Steering Committee, both the Teacher Liaison and the Head Teachers' Committees (both greatly extended) remain at post.

The debate continued. We were looking for points of leverage or purchase for the project; we were probing for openings and seeking for opportunities. The horn of the dilemma, namely, that Educational Priority Areas should have schools different in kind, was not baldly put. The idea was raised as a stalking-horse and sometimes as a long-term vision. In effect, we argued, this might be the future ideal, but given the rather shattering reality of the present, it might still be possible to take a hesitant step or two in that direction. To inaugurate practical discussion, we intimated that each school might mount exploratory probes in the curriculum and in home and school links and possibly in opening out the school and its activities to the community at large.

Gradually a nexus of action along these lines was negotiated. It was hoped that this would enliven the climate and life of the schools, incorporating a reappraisal of school aims and content in terms of their relevancy and satisfaction for the urban child. This was our touchstone: the adaptation of the curriculum to meet the immediate everyday needs of the urban child. Beyond that we saw an opportunity of encouraging teachers to re-evaluate sights and objectives and of quickening parental interest in terms of less alienation from the substance and attitudes of school-life. We finally looked for an involvement of community and school at various levels for the social benefit of both. In that our overview was the theme of the Community School, the elements fitted neatly. A Community School should perhaps have a 'community' curriculum, as a pivot for teachers, children, parents and community at large.

The curriculum explorations ran the gamut of the normal primary school timetable. The schools' reasons for wishing to try particular items varied. Some wished to boost a part of the syllabus that appeared to be successful, whereas others wished to turn their hand to an aspect under-played in the school. This did not, of course, affect the common issue which the project team wished to examine. In reality, the question asked of each probe was: to what extent does the urban child derive immediate satisfaction or day by day value from this piece of work. Anxious to see the community school as a unified process, geared to daily life and freed from academic abstracts, there was another criterion. We wanted to see how far an especial curricular item led to an integration of school-work, and whether, at best, a single point of departure might not be sufficient unto the day, thereby making ordinary syllabus considerations redundant. Few teachers would accept the extremity of the argument. It was hard to accept that immediate joys should never give way to the hierarchical development of knowledge or that hitherto critical material might be omitted through full-scale integration. But many already operated, of course, degrees of child-centredness, in regard both of attitude and substance. Probably the most difficult concept to accept was that of relevance, that curricular content might change drastically according to area, and that it should be adjudged sound, not only in interesting the child, but in specifically serving his social education.

Eventually, about nine curricular probes were agreed. They included two specifically infant schemes, one in language and one in number; another two in environmental familiarization and in mathematics, bestrode the infant and junior worlds; and the remainder were principally junior. They sought to examine leisure pursuits, the local environment, cultural 'stimulation', creative expression and animal and plant life for the 'downtown' juniors. These nine probes in the project schools were the first part of the programme to be decided and the first to be underway. The home or community and school links were again varied to give the project team a breadth of experimentation. We decided to lend support and thus to look for guidance in two parental groups, neither of which had a formal structure. Parents were invited during school-time, sometimes the total parent body, sometimes a class group, to a series of activities. These were part-educative and part-social. Many combined the two. For instance, a demonstration of low-budget cookery or clothes-making had an entertainment and a utility element. We also wanted to try publications from school to home, and we were lucky to obtain help from the Liverpool Regional College of Art in the presentation of these. They were a prospectus for parents and intending parents, a periodic newsletter, consisting of information about school activities and methods, and a periodic magazine of children's and, it was hoped, parents' contributions. It was also intended to follow up the receipt of these publications. There was next the improvement of amenities, such as murals and garden baskets in a school playground or the reclamation of part of a school site as a tiny park. There was an attempt to reach the community by exhibitions of school work in those natural foci of school and society, the local shops. All of them were developed by the children. It was seen basically as the children, in these varied ways, approaching the community and developing links with its differing elements.

It should be stressed that these score or so mini-projects were feasibility studies. They were to be attempted in order to assess which were most useful, that these few might be reinforced either in depth or by transfer to other schools. Those that proved unsuccessful were allowed to run out their own natural course. Moreover, the division of the topics into 'curricular' or 'parental/community' gives something of a false picture, for it was intended that, in a given situation, they would interact. For example, the school with the animal and plant-life project would use the material as the base for its magazine and for its shop exhibition.

The programme: Pre-school provision

So far the programme was oriented to the primary school, but it was well-received that pre-school provision was grossly inadequate in the educational priority zone. Here the question was whether there was any, rather than, as with the primary school, how was it done. It was decided that we should examine the mechanics of extending the provision through the mobilization of community resources. To this end we hoped to start a number of play-groups, but by and large, our major intention was to improve the quality and quantity of the existing pattern of playgroups.

Local feeling we found to be most sympathetic towards our view, and the LEA generously agreed to pay the salaries of part-time helpers although supply of such staff was very overstretched and, in fact, only two were recruited. We hoped to observe the playgroup attached to the primary school, with mother participation; the playgroup attached to the secondary school with senior pupil participation; the playground in the industrial or commercial context; the playgroup in concert with the neighbourhood association of which several existed in the EPA; as well as the playgroup with a more orthodox private or church basis. Other thoughts that occurred to us were the compilation of 'instant' plays kits, in lockable boxes on castors which, themselves, became component parts. These were to build up commercially, but we also hoped to encourage fresh designs for playgroup kits, suited especially to the urban child. Another idea was the use of a mobile pre-school unit, and here we planned to renovate a double-decker bus, which we arranged to obtain from the corporation transport department. It was felt that, after the precedent of Mahomet and the mountain, that this might have some value in an urban community.

There is little doubt that this side of the programme, despite the enormous sympathy it evoked, was slow to develop. Little, if any, of it was new, but the construction from scratch of playgroups (as opposed to the purely internal modifications we were inaugurating in ongoing institutions like the primary schools) was a lengthy process. Along with the problems of premises, supervisors, equipment and so on, there was also a problem of clientele. For instance, an afternoon session for a pre-school child could mean a mother, perhaps with children under four as well, making four journeys. Pre-school does not give the release to the mother that the full school day offers, especially when the child can travel under his own steam. Whatever its purpose for the child it can, paradoxically, add a further onus to a mother's overburdened day.

The most significant idea to arise was the idea of a playgroups' federation. It was splendid for the brash young men from the government to start brand new playgroups, but the effect of this on the morale of the poor mothers and social workers who had been struggling to make ends meet for years, was likely to be harmful. Out of a series of meetings arranged in concert with Phil Doran, then the Area Community Warden, the Liverpool EPA

Playgroups' Association emerged, manifesting the rather non-maternal abbreviation EPA PA. It was salutary to watch this emergent collective. When, at early meetings, there was talk of constitutions and legal footings, interest waned. The motives of the mothers and playgroup leader attending was uncompromising. They wanted better playgroups. The intricacies of democratic rigmarole moved them but slightly: had the most tyranically-minded Sultan offered his patronage to the association, they would have accepted it eagerly. When meetings became financially and practically oriented, interest waxed. It was salutary, too, to note the reaction to the professionals, like ourselves, who attended. The theory of social worker non-intervention and the spontaneous contribution of unimposed patterns of community behaviour look liberal and well-intentioned. In this company, the professionals were men in suits drawing good salaries; they were human beings in the same situation, and they were expected to give a lead and not wait for some scouse Jeanne d'Arc to raise the pre-school banner. It could be that opting out, the other extreme from imposing professional, sometimes patronizing, solutions on residents, creates just as much a bar. Maybe visiting professionals and residents are, at those points in time, both members of the same community with similar rights and values.

As it was, EPA PA grew in wisdom and stature, and remained, beyond the project, as one of the lynchpins in the machinery of management and inter-communication we had endeavoured to create.

The programme: The secondary school

Having considered the pre-school and primary child, we could hardly omit some discussion of the secondary. Despite the project's Plowden derivation, the attempt to view the problem communally implied a necessary consideration of the adolescent alongside the other chronological stages. Housed, as we were, in the local Comprehensive School, it seemed wise to explore possibilities there, the more so as our project schools were mainly feeders of the school. The fact that, five months after the opening of the project, one of the teachers still regarded me as the school electrician was something of a spur to create a presence in the school. We were interested in the overlap of primary and secondary work, particularly where it affected the 'communal' character of the curriculum. As the school was barely older than the project, it would have been invidious to advise on adaptations before the school had settled in its own course, and, naturally, we were under some obligation to begin operations in the primary sectors. However, we opened negotiations with the head of the school, Ken Vaux, who from the beginning proved to be a steadfast and everhelpful friend to the project.

It was strongly urged that some social or communal practices should be included in the curriculum, and that the project would help to pursue these. Our view was similar to our attitude to primary education. The school and its work should be related directly and purposefully to its community for their mutual benefit. The advantage of a more mature age (it was often said to us that primary children were too young for social education) was probably cancelled by the encroachments of examination requirements. A notable national feature of community education in the secondary schools has been its relegation to extramural activity or to 'Newsom' projects for the purportedly less able to less examinable pupils. The project team's contention was that communal education was educational in its own right. In illustration, it could be argued that a group of children organizing an old people's club are not just doing the pensioners a service, they are able intelligently to relate history, domestic science, English, music, art, drama, technical subjects etcetera, around the activity and to invest them with the stimulus of a relevant purpose. The integrative nature of such propositions raised another obstacle in the secondary school, where custom demands a subject-centred timetable. As against the cohesive unity of the junior school class, the fragmentation of the secondary school day by period and by subject was obviously a difficulty.

Nonetheless, there was some desire to participate in the project, and it was interesting how the first topics arose from other parts of the programme: the home management department was happy to launch a pre-school playgroup and the technical department was pleased to modify the bus for use as a mobile pre-school unit. Other departments were keen to experiment, either in direct social service or, through music and other creative sub-

jects, in what might be called aesthetic welfare. Another meaningful factor was the external portrayal of the school in its very
sizeable catchment district. It was necessary to take the school to
the community, with the children prepared to exhibit their work
in a host of styles. The project was prepared to lend assistance here
on the hypothesis that the community school should not only
attract people in, but should go out to the people.

Adult education

This left the highly significant adult sphere, and the early reconnaissance here suggested a firm linkage with the rest of the programme. It seemed that the EPA adult's need was the skill to
grapple with his social problems, for it was a fair assumption that
his schooling had not helped him overmuch in this direction.
Thus, adult education could be seen as a kind of remedial community education, making good the lack of skills previously
taught, in terms of communal participation. One aspect was the
parental one and the need to assist parents to understand their
children's education that they might the better support their own
children's efforts. It soon became obvious to Tom Lovett that the
style of approach most suitable in the socially disadvantaged districts was not unlike that found most beneficial in EPA primary
schooling. All this served to give a welcome unity, purpose and
format to the project as it endeavoured to establish its womb-to-
tomb spectrum.

Alongside this very brief introduction to the complex issue of
adult education in EPAs, one might also mention two other
communal slants we were hopeful of investigating. One was the
place of the economy in what might be called the extended community. In thinking of school and community, the residential
surrounds of the school are usually imagined, but the economic
sector is an equally vital one. We were concerned then, with the
validity of education in the sense of the pupil's adjustment to his
economic life and with the need for education and the economy
to relate more intimately. As Tom Ward, a shrewd and highly
socially conscious business-executive on our Local Steering
Committee, remarked: 'Your output is our input.' The other was
school management. It was imperative that, if school management was going to survive the onset of community schooling in a

utilitarian fashion, both its structure and function had to be altered. We intended to investigate the type and method of management needed to ensure that the school manager or governor could positively act as a bridge between school and community, an interpreter of one to the other.

But it was the general issue of adult education which caused most impact and it soon became apparent that Tom Lovett's pioneering work was to be as meaningful in its ramifications as any other in the project. His acute perception of the need to turn to non-formal social groups, in pubs and community centres, at home and at the school gate, and to adapt something like the primary school 'discovery' method in an effort to draw them into dialogue and self-diagnosis of educational need and possible provision – this was a component of the project which enabled it properly to boast of a cradle to grave range. The acceptance of popular culture and the mass media as automatic choices for the content and relaying of adult education conjoined with the productive character of these non-formal approaches to establish a cross-section of adult groups. At the peak of the season there would perhaps be twenty or so of these operating, and they balanced well with the thirty or so playgroups which made up the EPA Playgroups' Association. It was with some pride that I observed the creation of a kind of educational sandwich, with sound pre-school and adult educational experiments on either side of our more conventional school activities.

The programme: The colleges of education

Little mention has yet been made of the Colleges of Education to whom we paid the compliment of touring them as soon as our initial round of school visits was completed. There were ten colleges in the Liverpool Area Training Organization, only one of them so far removed in distance from the EPA as to be all but inaccessible. Two of the colleges were specialist colleges, with a secondary bias, and, as we were approaching all of them part-way through an academic year when plans were well laid, there were bound to be obstacles. Nonetheless, there was in the main a noble response to our call for help. We asked for tutor-led student teams to assist with the primary school projects, as well as giving the Research Officer help with collation of school and community data and lending support to some pre-school groups. We hoped their involvement would be double-edged, with a student (usually allocated to a small group of children) backing the curricular work and also evaluating its effects on the children. Just as we had formed a Teacher Liaison Group, we soon established a College Tutor Liaison Group, which met once or twice a term to swap ideas and exchange notes. One of its initial tasks was to attach particular colleges to particular schools, and this was done informally, according to college interests and previous connections.

The colleges were perceptive enough to realize that we did not approach them cap-in-hand, but that we were offering a unique opportunity for engagement in a national project. We earnestly requested that, where possible, students should be deployed on a regular, intramural basis, rather than out of goodwill in free time. This was meant kindly towards the students, who the project team felt should see attachment to our work as an integral part of their course. By modifying school practice requirements and special study commitments to the realistic material of a government project, one hoped to give the students a worthwhile educative experience. In terms of the EPA dilemma, the pay-off for teacher-education could well be significant. Teacher-education is, naturally enough, a link in the circle of events that makes the education system in a priority area what it is. Many college tutors were keen to join in with the project work in order to appreciate the more the situations for which they were preparing teachers. Few of them would perhaps have gone to the extreme where it was implied that if EPAs demanded different schools, they would require different teachers. But they took the point that colleges had a major role to play in any future development in EPA education.

The college teams were manned and posted with alacrity, and by February of 1969 most schools and colleges were in action. The opening months were profitably used to establish the human rapport and, on the basis of practical experience, to iron out snags and frame realistic programmes. One factor emerged very clearly during this initial stage. It was apparent that, irrespective of the actual substance of the projects, the relation of college and school was going to prove rewarding in its own right. Tutors soon began to spot profitable approaches; students began to enjoy the regular contact with the school; teachers found refreshment and support in their presence; and, as one head teacher commented, for the first time in his experience the children stopped regarding the students as students. Of course, there were ripples in the smooth pattern, but, on the whole the atmosphere of the college-school association was fine, and it was good to watch, for example, tutors re-thinking traditional modes of school attachment.

In brief, what the Plowden Report called 'a continuing link' between colleges and EPA schools became a much larger section of the project than had originally been planned. One saw that our conclusions would include important recommendations about this aspect. This immediately met the criticism levelled at the concept of college attachment that it was luxurious and could not be made general practice. A quick calculation of the strength of colleges on Merseyside against the designated EPA schools revealed that association of this kind would not prove onerous. It could help to meet the teachers' point made over and over again that all the EPA schools really need is a better staffing ratio.

The College Tutor Liaison Group was the fifth and last of our management structures. It worked immensely hard throughout the project to strengthen the links of school and college, but the administrative pitfalls involved in gearing colleges to the challenge and making in-roads into entrenched timetables and academic positions consumed too much time. It meant that too little space was afforded the tutors for exchanging information about the work the students and schools were doing. It meant that the business of petty administration blocked a proper debate as to the principles of teacher-education that were now being questioned. It took almost three years of hard forging before these long-term educational matters were validly aired. Nonetheless, the College Tutor Group became, on balance, more institutionalized than the other bodies, with its own chairman and secretary. It worked through from a college mart providing twelve schools with college teams on an ad hoc basis to a well-organized agency tooling up thirty schools with college teams numbering as many as three hundred students in total. The formalization of the College Tutors Group was the first happy indication of continuity, and, by the end of the second year, I was assured that here was one innovation which would remain permanent. In turn, the Playgroups Federation, the Headteachers Standing Committee, the Teacher Liaison Committee, and, most meaningfully, the Local Steering Committee, agreed to remain in being, and it was on that network of intercommunication that the future progress of the project rested.

It was interesting to look back in retrospect from these palmy days of happy relationship between the colleges and so many schools, to those early times when, naturally, there was a little suspicion on the schools' side and a little gaucherie on the colleges' side. We acted as a marriage bureau for school and college. There was never exactly a shotgun marriage, but some parties came reluctantly and hesitatingly to the ceremony. A lengthy round of such educational nuptials was assuredly one of the most tiring parts of the work. Keith Pulham will recall emerging with me from one such negotiation, and, in a mixture of relief and relaxation, we played football with a piece of polystyrene in Lime Street.

The general strategy

This, then, was the general outline of the approach. As the Liverpool EPA presented such an interwoven complex of multi-deprivation and as project teams had been urged nationally to examine the problems communally, it seemed neither possible nor helpful to separate the strands of special need. The problem was approached as one of an entire community at social and educational risk. This was a community in transition, and our general commitment to education and this community, as opposed to a specific treatment of especial cases, led us to consider a strategy of action in breadth.

Other reasons for so doing materialized during the reconnaissance period. Firstly, it seemed risky to pour resources wholesale into one or two schemes, in case these turned out wasteful. It seemed wiser to take soundings on a wide front in order that, as some might appear more feasible than others, they could be further backed. Secondly, the EPA school exists on a psychological and social cliff-edge, and the slightest dislocation can disrupt it. Thus, one must move gingerly, attempting small-scale innovation and using latent interest, for what may seem tiny on a national perspective can look monstrous to the EPA school. Thirdly, many of the powers-that-be are not able to interest themselves in expensive schedules, and it seemed that economic and tactical investment might prove more helpful to them than extravagant successes too exorbitantly priced to be copies.

An outline of the commitments made by various organizations is, in part, a catalogue of the resources afforded the project. There was the substantial amount in kind from the local education authority (after all, we had what amounted to offices and full services in the city centre which must have amounted to thousands of pounds over the three year period), there was the build-up of staff and our own salaries to be found. The critical finances were the actual governmental funds for running the project, and these amounted to £21,000 over three and a third years, that is, ten terms: £2,100 a term; £17 for each day. Inflation (especially in transport and printing costs) hit us harshly over the period, and £17 was, for instance, 35p a day for each Liverpool EPA school. It was hardly a princely sum to embark on a revolutionary appraisal of urban education. A rough analysis of expenditure suggests an approximate break-down as follows: retaining fees and additional salaries, 10%; production of curriculum kits and publications generally, 20%; pre-school, secondary, adult education and miscellaneous ventures, 20%; primary school curricular development and home/school relations, 50%. This, of course, reflected the Plowden primary school orientation of the project.

The incidence of expenditure also illustrated the approach we were practising. Apart from the development of a number of curriculum kits, we kept much of our spending down to the kind of sums which were likely to be replicable. Ten pounds here and twenty-five pounds there was much more likely to impress the administrators faced with stringent fiscal regulos.

Beyond that, finance was an enabler. Our essential task was to lubricate schools and other agencies in order that they might attempt the attitudinal changes which were necessary. Often, we enabled teachers to try experiments that lack of small sums had hitherto prevented. We were also concerned to draw the teachers and others into a willing and cooperative entity. One is not

ashamed to admit that certain expenses were defrayed for social-
izing. Teachers' luncheons, end-of-term parties, a glorious old
time music-hall, complete with jellied eels and pork pies and the
Paddington School band – these are instances of the cheerful
social life we tried to float. It helped raise morale; it kept a large
team involved and intact and it gave a measure of pleasurable
import to teachers too long ignored. It had more tangible
rewards. Time and again teachers and heads reminded us that,
without such a social calendar, they often remained apart and
thus incommunicado. Many ideas were thrashed out and many
activities transferred from school to school over the excellent
lunches provided by Paddington's first-class home management
department.

Such wining and dining is part and parcel of action-research.
It may sound trivial, even extravagant, but the truth is that we
had to care for our participating parties if we expected them to
care for us. That is not to say that we approached the project's
social whirl in a mood of utility; they were happy years, with
plenty of achievement, challenge and genial good humour to be
shared by everyone.

Another example of the lubricant nature of money is its deployment for goodwill. Very quickly, in action-research programmes, does one have to show willing. Within weeks, one is
being asked when resources are to become available, and it is a
fair question. There have been too many long looks and low
outcomes in deprived areas. We had, in a graphic phrase we
coined, to show blood on the snow.

All these instances recall that it was an exercise in diplomacy,
rather than scholarship. We constantly walked a diplomatic
tightrope. There were cases where a year's hard work to create
goodwill was invalidated by five minutes' trouble or error. In
vain might one ask for the twelve months' guiltless period to be
considered; the evil lived on, the good was interred. It was what
we christened the Tallyrand–Blondin syndrome, the perpetual
and vigilant watch for possible causes of friction or difficulty as
we endeavoured to survive and advance on that slender line between success and failure.

There were certain implications raised by this avowal that the
task was more a political than an academic exercise. It meant

that, in effect, the Liverpool project did less pure academic research than any of the other projects. It also meant that we found it valuable to begin with a broadscale assault on the problem and, indeed, to treble the number of schools in which we eventually operated. It further meant that it was always our intention to keep the problem alive. It was imperative to maintain the EPA problem constantly in the public eye, and this, we felt to be part of our job. Not everyone agreed with us, preferring a more scholarly and pacific attitude, and this was obviously a sensitive area. Nonetheless, it is fair to argue that three of the several reasons why the Liverpool project was the only one to remain in united being were . . . the emphasis on action, the wide range of endeavour and the publicity received.

Throughout the three years of the project we received, in terms relative to like agencies, a certain amount of journalistic and televisual coverage. We also tried our own brand of publicity through our house journal, *Projectile*, and a series of ten occasional papers, now published in book form.* Each time we publicized, we took a calculated gamble, especially when television was the medium. In order to demonstrate an answer to a problem, it was, of course, necessary to expose the nature of the problem, and it was often felt that the exposure was rather overdone as opposed to the thin treatment of positive solutions. It is true that bad news is good news and that dereliction and other troubles made for more stunning pictures and copy than the less vivid shots and descriptions of teachers and parents working hard to put these things right. However correct we felt the balance had been attained, there were inevitably complaints; certainly no television items, whether magazine spots or full length programmes, escaped without our being faced with criticisms of distortion or shortselling. The normal production business of long takes and brief flashes, even non-appearances, were always calculated to annoy. Sometimes we considered lengthily and seriously whether to continue such coverage.

But one invariably returned to the point where a socially disadvantaged citizenry and its hard-pressed teachers have been badly served by non-publicity and the sweeping of the social dust

* *Projections*, ed. Eric Midwinter, Ward Lock Educational (1972).

under the carpet. It is a matter of opinion whether publicity helps or not. My own view was that, whilst each individual article or item might not produce a sparkling reaction, there was a gradual accretion of general knowledge about the severity of the problem and the character of the answers proposed. One must not allow this particular question to get out of hand. At the end of three years there were teachers, never mind parents, living within sight of the Liverpool EPA who didn't know of our existence. We had neither the time nor the resources to embark on a massive selling campaign, nor were our activities colourful and newsworthy. Still, when chance offered, we judged it right to broadcast the case of the Educational Priority Area.

I have tried to describe the complicated process of building up a programme of action alongside a structure for action. The two were so interconnected that it is difficult to analyse them separately. The type of action required dictated the managerial form erected. It was important to understand not only what needed to be done and whether people agreed it should be done; it was equally important to know how it could be done and to persuade people to do it. One had to build a programme of activities which, conceivably, might later emerge as a rarefied formula for community schooling, all of which met broadly the theoretical criteria of community education, and which was, by and large, agreed by the participants. At the same time, one had to commit, physically, emotionally and morally, as many people as possible to the ideal of the urban Community School, so that a task-force was recruited actually to undertake the operation. In turn, one had to assess the effect of each piece of action and the character and commitment of each participant on both the remainder of the programme and the rest of the people engaged thereon, in a kind of criss-cross foursome. This mixture of personalities and purposes was a volatile broth. Stirring it and watching it was an arduous culinary experience. It was sweated labour. It was like slaving over a hot stove for three years. Luckily, the proof of the pudding lies in the eating, and the success of the project, insofar as it remains in business, was its own reward.

So the project began. It would be foolish to pretend that the mood of the project team was other than pessimistic. The problems and issues seemed gargantuan in every way, whereas the

resources of time, manpower and money were correspondingly
puny. Nevertheless, the spirit was one of cheerful pessimism, a
feeling that it was essential and worthwhile to make the attempt.
One recalled the prayer of the grizzled Yorkshire senior professional before a vital 'Roses' match at Old Trafford: 'Oh, Lord,
tha knows and ah knows that if tha wants them to win, they'll
win, and if tha wants us to win, we'll win; but if you could just
keep out of it for three days, we'll thrash hell out of them.'
Against the sombre nature of the problem, our meagre
opportunity seemed as three days set against eternity, but we
hoped to make the best of it.

5 The Action 1
The Project at Work

The action initiated during the opening year (that is, from January to the summer of 1969) clearly illustrated the point that innovation is a form of reconnaissance. By attempting a wide-ranging series of explorations, we were able, by the beginning of the academic year 1969–70, to lay down a rather more structured programme. A six months' flurry of energetic activity proved of enormous value. It enabled judgements to be made about the viability of hitherto theoretical ideas, the strengths and weaknesses of the outline schedule, the temper and character of the people and institutions under consideration and the multitude of snags that needed to be ironed out before a more thorough-going programme was possible.

In this, as in all the other aspects of the work, the notion of the multiplier was to the fore, in terms both of sustaining the project beyond its three-year time-span and of expanding it geographically. The action-research project is, as Francis Bacon said of money, 'lyke unto muck, no good lest yt be spread.' More and more we came to believe that the visible or demonstrable practice of action-research is, in itself, as valuable a means of communicating results as reportage and that one yardstick of success is the notice taken of such visible practice. Action thus becomes its own research.

Apropos this and the urgent need to keep the EPA problem in the public eye, the end of the first year produced a veritable plethora of welcome and, in the main, favourable publicity as people began to wonder how affairs were going after the opening months of the project. The disadvantage of action-research is that growth is a chief measure of success and that, as the project grew, it took on some of the attributes of a Frankenstein. One example of this was that people began to use the project as a posting-box for items which did not quite fit in elsewhere. One ruefully recalled the circus performer who sets plates whirling on the top of twenty or thirty canes and then races around to keep them whirling. The project action had something of this quality of an unceasing gallop to keep too many schemes alive and kicking. It was apparent even after six months that the major goals of the project were now more discernible than when, at first, we embarked on our so-called philosophic inquiry. The feeling of the project team had hardened in favour of a differentiated, rather than a compensatory, form of education in the EPA. The early musings about the common format of the education system had developed into a more critical approach as the daily observation of its defects drove the lesson home. This heightened regard for schools, differing in pattern and content as their catchment areas prescribed, evolved, vis-à-vis the establishment of a more definitive view of the community school, as one in which school and community interlocked closely for mutual benefit. This implied that the community school must vary according to the dictates of its surrounds. Thus, on both grounds, the idea of an EPA Community School, distinct in character from other schools, became clearer.

In turn, this enabled the project team to clarify aims and these were twofold. Firstly, it seemed likely that, drawing on the broad-scale experience from our several schools, we would arrive at a series of definitions about the EPA Community School and of recommendations about its practical implementation. These could be selected and modified, according to circumstance and predilection, at all levels, from national or local administrative circles to the headteacher in the school and the teacher in the classroom. Secondly, it seemed possible that this series of recommendations would also furnish the hypotheses for long-term, concrete proposals, possibly with a more puristic research element. For instance, firm proposals about a purpose-built EPA Community School or for alterations in teacher-education might be laid. We were very conscious of the sheer lack of hypotheses for attacking the system at its base, as opposed to its superstructure, which is the more usual target of educational research. There was a clear necessity for action programmes designed to stir up new thoughts, appraisals and approaches. The long-term goal of establishing the Community School was clear enough. In our view, the Community School is essential in all areas; by the end of year one, we wondered whether, in Educational Priority Areas, it might well be a matter of life or death.

In the second year we consolidated the probings and explorations of the first year into a much more well-defined schedule of operations. On the one side, some of the original ideas had come to nothing; on the other side, some had proved fruitful enough to spread to other schools, so that, during the second year, several schools adopted additional measures and began to stoke up their community schooling practice. By the end of the critical second year, twelve of the thirteen school departments where we began work were buzzing industriously on our behalf and just one had rather fallen by the wayside. This last was a case where, after what seemed useful beginnings in the first year with a college attachment, some interesting curricular work and a sound home/school publication, the headteacher obviously felt that this kind of activity was perhaps inhibiting the normal emphasis of the school which was geared very firmly to language teaching. It's pleasing to add that there was no strain in relations between the school and the project; merely a respected decision, that the school could not 'take' the project approach. It was a disappointment, but it was the only major setback we suffered among the schools, and that without rancour or difficulty. The pre-school, adult and miscellaneous schemes were also prospering soundly. It was a year of phenomenal activity and the productivity rates were very high. It was in this year that the main meat of the project became available.

Consolidation was the key to the third year. It was now known that the project would be, in some form, sustained, and that the LEA intended to take a lively interest in its survival. It was also felt that as solid a base as possible must be laid for the advance of community education in the Liverpool EPA, and that the obligations of action-research involved some attempt to assure that whatever had been successfully started could go on.

These arguments pointed to a policy of consolidation and retrenchment at all levels of the project. Two other arguments clinched the decision. The major administrative components, such as our teacher-education exercise, our pre-school federation and our adult programme, had enjoyed only a short life and another year of similar development was still no more than a brief experiment. Many of the networks of communication that had been laid required years of practice to see their most fruitful fulfilment. The third year was also a year of clarification and documentation, a year so replete with recording the past and preparing for the future that many new ventures were out of the question; a year, needless to say, in which project funds became shorter, not least as inflation and other factors drove up costs considerably.

Perhaps the outstanding example of consolidation was the decision to earmark a sum of £1,500 for the original project schools to continue their project work. After detailed negotiations, estimates were drawn up for each of the school departments initially engaged on the project and grants awarded accordingly. These varied from £50 to £300 depending on the size of the school and the extent of its project efforts. This worked admirably. It gave heads and staff an inkling of the costs of such exercises; it acted as a useful administrative aid to a project which had lost much time previously in a mass of petty accounting; it delineated a transitional stage between schools reliant entirely on project administration and schools with no project to support them; it made for speed of administration and a capacity for schools to meet quickly those contingencies that peculiarly afflict the EPA school; it offered evidence (were any needed) that schools are capable of handling rather larger sums than the somewhat trifling petty cash floats with which they are normally entrusted. There was not a hitch. Accounts were returned in due time, complete with valid certification.

By this stage there were several schools which had embarked on an ambitious programme of community schooling. Some schools had organized all-round programmes, with perhaps a magazine, parental at-homes, a site-improvement scheme, a curricular exploration and a student team. The headteachers were generous in their praise of the project – one of them claimed his school had been transformed by its presence – and they kindly volunteered to submit a favourable report on their findings to the LEA. Individually, they recorded their opinions, and then two of their number drew up a brief document which all but one signed, for submission to the Education Committee. If the proof of the project pudding be in the eating, this was a most signficant 'good food guide'.

Easily the single greatest innovation of the final year was the Project Extension Programme – 'Operation PEP'. This was intended to draw as many EPA schools as possible into the dubious embrace of the project, extending what was believed to be sound from our early experience to whichever EPA schools were interested. It was, in part, an effort to meet the needs of an Educational Priority *Area*, as opposed to a sample of its schools, and we tried to bear in mind that, at the end of the project, the LEA would be thinking in terms of offering treatment to all EPA schools and not just a sample: we were interested, therefore, in creating a climate of opinion in which such further action might propitiously be engendered. It was, in part, a rough and ready evaluation. Given two years hard labour in the area in a cross-section, geographically speaking of its schools, which ones, having watched and waited, would be prepared to join us?

Two letters were dispatched and a couple of meetings, one of representative teachers, one of heads, were held. We prepared and costed a schedule of activities and this included free gifts of all our 'Projector' work-kits and other literature, the promise of a student team and the offer of some or all of a 'communal' package of parental at-homes, publications, site-improvements and exhibitions. A small sum of £400 was all that could be afforded to meet the individual needs of this last item.

In the event, twenty-two schools agreed, in part or whole, to participate. Several of these, of course, were already doing similar work, but it was amazing how some of these schools reacted to Operation PEP. They stirringly answered the call and, in curricular as in parental activity, one or two wellnigh outstripped original 'project' schools of two years' standing.

The seventeen refusals were, naturally enough, our major concern and Keith Pulham carried out an intensive piece of research by interview as to why these school departments were not anxious to join the project. It must, in parenthesis, be noted that these seventeen school departments represented, in fact, only ten schools, given some of their division under independent heads into infants, junior boys and junior girls. Of the seventeen schools, fourteen were Roman Catholic, two were Church of England and only one was an LEA school.

Fifteen of the seventeen heads concerned were interviewed at length and only three felt the project had no value. Their reasons for non-commital were varied, but they may be roughly categorized under four headings. First, there were four heads who had never seen or had forgotten the letter. They were all new appointees. Two immediately decided to join the project – one with conspicuous success on the curricular front. Second, there were five heads, all of Catholic schools, who believed that material circumstances – awaiting rebuilding, cramped premises and so on – prevented their undertaking project work. Third, there were those who believed that the scheme was unnecessary in their schools. While approving of the EPA movement in principle, they felt it did not apply to them, such was the efficiency and success of their schools. Fourth, there were three Catholic heads who objected, on principle, to the EPA approach, regarding it respectively as 'bound to fail', as 'unnecessary in a good Catholic school' and as a 'hindrance'.

The first and last categories were, in their separate ways, straightforward. It is difficult to decide how valuable the middle two sets of comments were, with one group arguing cramped facilities and other adequate facilities as reasons as opposed to the direct objections of the fourth category. Another issue raised by this piece of research was the worry that some staffs were obviously not in contact with the project and that we were heavily reliant on heads for such publicity.

Given these assortments of motives, and with twenty-two schools willing to play, the project staff felt reasonably encouraged as they embarked on this new enterprise. It became Keith Pulham's main and awesome third year task to handle Operation PEP and to record its progress and this he did with characteristic tidiness and attention. It is to him we are indebted for the following analysis. It reveals that, of the twenty-two schools, all used 'Back Home' parents publication described later in this chapter (and several of them utilized it to very satisfying effect); twelve attempted some form of parental liaison on the 'coffee morning' pattern; eight tried site-improvement, chiefly playground wall mural schemes; two embarked on highly pleasing exhibitions in local shops; six contributed to our little festival, 'Cityscenes'; and eighteen enjoyed the help of student teams.

Even statistically, this was quite a good start. It might be worth mentioning at this juncture that, in our thirty-four 'project' and 'extension' schools, there were in that third year approaching thirty curriculum probes; nine individual publications, as well as a total utilization, with one exception, of our general 'Back Home' publication; nineteen schools with direct and regular parental link-up; sixteen schools with site-improvement schemes; three schools exhibiting in local shops; fourteen schools which contributed to our final year 'Cityscenes' exhibition; and some thirty college teams.

There were drawbacks. It was not a consistent pattern. Some of the twenty-two schools were working hard on project activities; others were doing so little they could hardly be counted. Occasionally, one was asked for money for objectives way outside the project brief, and there were, now and again, signs that the overview of community education was not fully accepted nor understood. Figures for parental at-homes did not seem so high in 'extension' schools as in one or two of the 'project' schools, even allowing for the latters' longer running activity. As ever, much was dependent on the appropriate head teacher; a change of head meant, in several cases, a fresh breeze blowing in favour of the project or (thankfully, less rarely) the reverse. It seemed that constant attention was necessary in several connections, and this a small project team could not always guarantee. With so many student teams, the quality and character of the college-school linkage also varied enormously, and some schools – and some students – felt that the gains had not been as good as they might have been.

Over against this rather confused picture of inconsistent, wide-ranging activity must be set the general point of climate. It can scarcely be gainsaid that, as a consequence of the Project Extension Programme, several more headteachers and many more teachers heard of and reacted appreciatively to the project, several hundreds of children, and many of their parents, received an educative-cum-social booster and a number of schools looked at themselves critically in the light of the standards of school and community. All this must be profit, especially in regard to an ongoing project in Liverpool, with its aim the promulgation of the Community School throughout the Educational Priority Area.

So much for a general overview of the three-year-plan and the strategy mounted to implement it. It is intended now to look in more detail at what transpired to be the six chief areas of concern, granting that this analysis into categories is a formal one for, at all times, their operations were interdependent. The six areas were: pre-school playgroup support, the community-oriented curriculum and home or community and school relations (these two together forming the core of our schools' programme), adult education, continuing links with colleges of education, and the secondary field.

Pre-school provision

Our pre-school campaign to extend provision in an area of severe short-fall was slow to mature and was proved inordinately ambitious. We helped to initiate four playgroups of different types, of which the ones started in a primary school, with reception staff help, and in a secondary school, with senior pupil help, were outstandingly successful. But it was a disappointing start. At best, no more than sixty children were newly involved in pre-school provision and it was ominous that, in each of the three operational cases, the existence of an ongoing institution and qualified staff was crucial. The LEA had generously permitted us to employ, at their expense, up to six half-time staff, but, so tightly stretched was pre-school staffing, only one suitable person had been found until, in the last year of the project, another assistant was appointed. The early six months' trial period also emphasized the folly of a tiny project team embarking on a major provision programme while, at the same time, organizing fair-sized activities in other fields. It had been a Canute-like gesture. A combine of virtue and necessity thus prevailed on us to exchange our policy of provision for one of support and we attempted to draw all the playgroups in the locality into a loose federation for mutual benefit. It was strongly felt that the solidarity of such a federation would improve both the quantity and quality of pre-school provision through the sharing of ideas, fund-raising, equipment, bulk purchasing, training management and sheer friendship in what is too frequently an isolated situation. The project felt able to do four things. It made available £1,000 to support this experimental association, hopeful of passing much of the responsibility of its spending to the group leaders. This was a simple exercise in educational management; how economically can £1,000 be spent on playgroups in a given area? A survey of the 20-odd groups in the area was undertaken and this outlined the fabric and character of each group with valuable clarity, while Keith Pulham organized a pre-school parental survey with a view to assessing specific requirements. This excellent piece of research was to be of great use in future developments.

Thus, the pre-school action revolved around the development of the Liverpool EPA Playgroups Association and the urban rides of the Paddington playmobile, described in the next chapter.

The EPA PA immediately reaped psychological and physical rewards. Once a simple, workable constitution had been negotiated, the group began to use its monthly meetings for educative purposes, at the same time directly breaking down the isolated feeling that is the vocational hazard of the struggling playgroup leader. The togetherness of searching out answers to common problems proved very popular. A note of the initial four in this series must suffice as illustration. At the first, the local supervisor of the Save The Children Fund Playgroups, led a discussion based on art and craft work done in the different EPA playgroups. At the second, a local tutor spoke of the difficulties of music in the playgroup, an element probably as lacking as any in most of these situations. There was a guitar lesson, advice on songs and suggestions about percussion and other instruments. The third was a 'catalogue' evening, when catalogues were examined, partly as an educational operation and partly, through negotiating bulk purchase, an economic one. The fourth was on children's books, given by a children's librarian who wished to follow up with a 'book group' on a regular basis. These meetings remained informal and with the minimum of procedure. Increased numbers at each meeting told its own tale, as audiences began to push over forty. It was decided early on to involve parents more in these most interesting get-togethers and individual groups began to take it in turns to provide rather more lavish refreshments. In brief, the task of raising the quality of playgroup education was well under way, not least of all due to the eager recognition of this need by the playgroup ladies themselves.

The physical element – equipment and sources of supply continued to be the burning question, with shortage of cash always a problem. The EPA PA had long debates, both in committee and in plenary session, on how best the £1,000 project grant might be used. It was encouraging to observe a strong feeling for the 'under-privileged' playgroups and an equally pleasing sentiment in favour of welcoming and assisting new members to the Federation. The association soon remarkably had twenty-seven of the twenty-eight groups in the area as members, of which were four recently formed. Mrs Connor quickly built up a store of supplies at bulk and cut rates, and one of the association's first decisions was to allot a five pound voucher to each member group to be exchanged for such supplies. With a score of playgroups at varying levels of need and development, it was necessary to resolve some balance between a simple division of resources on a pro rata base and the absolute distribution of resources to those in dire need. The five pound voucher was a measure of this judicial principle; everyone immediately benefited from the idea of federation, but plenty was left in reserve for emergencies and distressed cases. The supervisors, who had often spent years living off a shoestring, were naturally adept in their agile utilization of their gift voucher, but it was also of interest to notice how the storeroom itself took on an educative mode. Novel materials on display can engineer new attitudes. 'Tissue paper', said one girl, rooting through the store, 'what can you do with that?' Within minutes, she bought some.

The value of the federation is obvious enough. The question is really one of mechanics. Two points are clear. One, the activity has to be directly and immediately valuable. At one stage, we found ourselves a trifle bogged down in the arduous democratic task of setting the association on some kind of constitutional foundation. Interest flagged, only to be spurred on when guitars, catalogues and vouchers were in the air. It is ruthlessly a utilitarian association with the members uncomplicatedly free from the procedural worries that occasionally stymie many institutions from the local tennis club to the House of Commons. Simply, it is done for the children's benefit and this mutual concern makes a loose informal structure desirable and inevitable. Two, the presence of a full-time worker in the shape of Mrs Connor has been indispensable, for this is a haphazard pattern of playgroups with no structural links save those formed by the supervisors and mothers. Arranging meetings and booking speakers, negotiating block purchasing, supervising storage, sales and accounts, regularly visiting to advise and encourage, organizing student support (several of the playgroups now have constant nursery student assistance), Eleanor Connor has successfully channelled the original impetus for federation single-handed. It is estimated that, in pyramidical style, she influences, like some glorified nursery headmistress, the educational lives of well over 500 children through EPA PA.

Turning to a final score point — the utilization of systematic teaching material in pre-school activity — the project produced a pre-school language kit. The EPA Projects experimented nationally with the American Peabody Kit and the results had been mildly encouraging in terms of improved linguistic performance. Apart from a traditional contempt in some quarters for any hint of programmed learning, other objectors had found fault with the American idiom of the Peabody Unit, which had been used in default of the existence of any like English kit. Beyond that, we were well aware of the vague and unco-ordinated nature of much pre-school playgroup work, particularly in language, in situations where organizers were scarce and overworked. As part of the project's general philosophy, there had been a strong commitment to relevancy in the curriculum, and there was some feeling that language materials at the under-five level were not much more realistic than for older children.

Everyone on the project turned a hand to producing this kit. On the basis of some national collations and the local testing for the Peabody experiment, we assembled a 'basic' vocabulary of 360 words we felt could be assumed; then, again using national norms, built up a 'new' vocabulary of 360 words. We then wrote twenty-four stories using the 360 words and with each story structured to introduce fifteen of the new words. An introductory manual explained the modus operandi; it included the two full lists of words, both alphabetically and by category, and it suggested how the story could be used and followed up in oral, artistic, musical and other ways over a week or a fortnight. The stories were accompanied by large wall illustrations and a puppet presenter, Dr Wotever, purportedly a local version of Dr Cameron, who was visiting the children and buttonholing them with a tale. The tales were set in and around a block of flats and chiefly concerned two small boys, Red Herring and Fynan Haddock, an old widow lady in one of the flats, Mrs Fluffffluff and the block carpenter, the irascible Mr Peppin. Mothers and supervisors were encouraged to use as much local reference as possible; there was nothing twee about the tales and it was hoped that infant reception classes might find a value in 'Wotever Next?', as the little kit was called. The enthusiasm with which it was initially received bespoke a crying shortage of materials, systematic but not inflexible, in playgroups. We made no great academic claim for the kit; it was an approximate attempt to offer a realistic and structured aid to the playgroup workers.

Primary school curriculum

Turning to the primary schools and the curriculum work they tried, nine probes, loosely geared to the concept of curricular relevancy, were started in the opening months. They existed in a free and easy atmosphere and no attempt was made to structure them. This came next. With some of the administrative snags and personality bumps dealt with, or, at least noted, it was now possible to programme a rather more purposive schedule, given also a firmer collegiate attachment. The major gain was an informed foundation on which to build a one-year curricular exploration in these situations. The normal structure was to suggest a list of termly or half-termly themes to be generally pursued by a class and with an intense emphasis during the weekly visit of the tutor-led student group. This involved most careful discussions among ourselves, headteachers, classteachers, tutors and students. It might be useful to present a summation of one or two of these explorations, normally using the reports kindly provided by the heads, teachers, tutors and students involved.

1. Junior maths and the environment: The supermarket

With the generous aid of Tesco Ltd, and numerous other firms, together with the splendid collations supplied by the pupils, a moderate-sized supermarket was simulated which quickly became the hub of the mathematical work. Two important reservations must be made; the maths was not exclusively supermarket (e.g. other mathematical experience was widely offered) and the supermarket was not exclusively maths (e.g. it led to varied social, creative and other studies). The supermarket was open to all the school, although, despite its size, only sections of a class could profitably use it at any one time, making 'student participation much appreciated'.

It became the most picturesque illustration of the community-oriented curriculum urged on schools by the project team. Its realism, its scope, its relevance and its attractiveness were seemingly inexhaustible. Its integrative character must especially be emphasized. It led, for instance, to children undertaking shop surveys, market research and so on. When a graph shows that the local shopping centre has eight chip shops and no bank, and when children begin to wonder why, the value of this kind of exercise takes on additional and meaningful dimension. It is difficult to overrate the value of this kind of real life exploration. Like an onion, the layers could be peeled off one by one. The maths and social studies apart, there existed the distinct scope for work in art and craft (the actual fabric of the store's surrounds, the window and shop displays, design of trading stamps and adverts) in several kinds of role-playing and in moral education, with issues such as shoplifting, advertising or smoking under discussion. It is probably not going too far to say that 'supermarket' fast became a subject.

The supermarket is but one possible simulation of this type. Other possibilities that spring to mind include the branch office of the Ministry of Social Security, the row of small specialist shops (perhaps one to each classroom; bank, travel agency, betting shop, newsagents, pub or snack bar, gas/electricity office, etc.) the clinic or surgery, the municipal agency (e.g. police, housing, welfare) and so on. The major point is to equip children to use (or avoid) everyday situations comfortably and critically;

the simulation is ideally suited to this kind of gentle testing or adaptation.

A 'shopping precinct' project was, in fact, inaugurated in another school. A large junior class and ten students set out to examine the local shopping scene. A student and three or four children chose a particular brand of shop and began to recreate it physically in the school. Slowly, a precinct – cards and sweets, flowers and plants, corner grocers and so on – grew, and very attractive it looked too. Verisimilitude, by the way of zebra crossings and so on, was added, and there was a café – the Sunshine Café – for the thirsty shopper. When all was complete, the parents were invited and the shops had products – made or grown by the children – to sell for the school funds, along with a drink and a bite to eat at the Sunshine Café. The children worked hard and enjoyed themselves; almost unwittingly, they involved every school subject, from craft and nature study to maths and cookery; in so doing, they discovered a tremendous amount about how the retail trade operates.

2. *Junior social environment: The locality*

The aim here was 'to heighten the child's awareness of his own environment, to utilize environmental features to help extend vocabulary, increase social awareness and promote interest in reading, number work and motor skills and to utilize environmental features as a basis for creative work'. The modus operandi was student-supervised exploration of the vicinity for purposes of sampling and collecting, followed by the utilization of such information in social and creative studies.

The student reports indicated the variety of environmental approaches tried. These included, on the basis of group outings, models of local factories and garages; a 'model' house with wallpaper, etc., designed by the children; work with road safety leading to the construction of an operable set of traffic lights and work on shape and measurement; mapping, direction-finding and routeing; the architecture and usage of local buildings, such as a nearby blood bank which entertained a student and her group of children to tea; social responsibility involving investigation of, for instance, the teamwork of the telephone exchange, especially in relationship to 999 calls; street surfaces with a careful examination of little-noticed features like hydrants, manhole covers and gas or electricity mains; street furniture, including the study of a rare pillar box eagerly sought after by hundreds of enthusiastic collectors; the derivation and meaningfulness of street names; and the changed utilization of buildings.

This is a random list. It merely illustrates what could contribute to a master-plan, a stout framework, allowing for much internal flexibility, by which a vicinity could be closely studied over a four-year junior range, drawing on all facets of experience, leading to all types of child activities and stimulating all manner of social familiarization. It was a most encouraging, far-reaching and pertinent endeavour. The students, like the tutors and teachers, felt the children had benefited, educationally and socially, during this second year stint. The work produced was certainly as varied as it was efficient and it was hard not to believe that the children were considerably 'socialized' as a consequence. One must mention Bobby, who, on completing a fine model of the new St John's Tower Restaurant in Liverpool, graphically described it as 'a chimney with a café on top'.

3. Junior social environment: Local amenities

In this case, the children studied their environment through the media of especial agencies or amenities. Once more, the aim was 'to make the children more aware of their surroundings: the amenities and lack of them, and for them to suggest ways of improvement.' Again, it was hoped 'to provide material for most subjects and to show how many interesting things children came into contact with in their everyday life.' The entire group, albeit, split into subgroups, according to a well-prepared schedule, took one topic at a time, the chief topics being the school, the church, the street and the home. These were each broken-down sector by sector for investigation by each student-led team.

Reports spoke of the increased conversational, written, artistic and social capacities of their charges and testified to the great enjoyment the children had found in the work. They also evidenced the immense variety of approach. To quote but one description of a term's work on 'the school', the five children in question used beads, matchboxes and drawings of children to graph aspects of the school, they completed a large pictorial graph showing the various types and shapes of rooms, they produced stories, drama and a collage, based on the use the school hall was put to and did some work on the properties of light, as it affected work in the school. It should be recalled that, at the end of each theme (usually lasting a term) the eight contributions were assembled into one unit, so that all the students and children could learn from and appreciate all the work.

To an outsider, the main impact was the quantity, as well as the quality, of the work. The actual amount of material imaginatively and competently presented was quite remarkable. Closer inspection revealed a most unremitting and detailed vigour in operation. The minute investigation of superficially humdrum items, like the different types of brickwork or windows in the school, was astonishing. It gave rise to interesting by-products; work on windows, led to a deeper study of glass and the construction of periscopes and mirrors. There could be little doubt that, in terms of skills' development and variety of experience, these themes were as exhilarating as any other and they carried with them the added bonus of a heightened awareness of the immediate surrounds. The dimensions of the academic assaults lifted them a full class above the normal, cheerfully haphazard centres of interest on 'our school' or 'our church'. They were indefatigable and uncompromising attempts to face local situations squarely and keenly.

4. *Junior leisure pursuits*

In this mini-project, the aim was straightforward enough. Given the evergrowing issue of leisure in its urban connotation, it was an attempt 'to offer the children a variety of activities not usually available in the school curriculum' in a fashion that might conceivably give them 'experience and interest to carry forward in their future life'. The student force, arguably, met the conventional counter to extended recreational opportunities that they cannot be explored in depth. The 'generous student/pupil allocation ensured the children received plenty of attention' and, after a week or so in which children shopped around these options, there was a settlement into a fairly well-defined pattern of activities.

The simplest description in this case is a straight catalogue of these options. They were: country dancing; film-making; mural-painting; rearing of indoor plants and animals (e.g. bottle gardens); ballet; dressmaking; fishing; needlework; piano-playing; woodwork; art; gardening; tennis; cookery; football; recorder-playing; athletics coaching; aeroplane modelling; and musical instrument-making. It is worth noting the overlap of project activities. The reclamation of a school garden and the later decision to undertake wall murals, initially inside the school, were ostensibly 'home and school' projects, but they naturally fitted into the gamut of leisure options. Two students and a group of interested children, for example, indulged their enthusiasm for gardening in this manner, while yet another student was busily producing a school magazine, drawing liberally on the work her confrères and their pupils were developing.

The diversity of activity was reflected in the diversity of opinion expressed. Perhaps predictably, there was a 'curate's egg' trait about this particular probe. Overall, the climate of this exploration was excellent and stimulating; more specifically, several of the individual pieces of work were enterprising, enjoyable and inventive – one could often sense lasting benefits being made. But, with such a welter of activities, there were two difficulties. One was that it could scarcely be expected that the students could all reach the same high level as some of their number, the more so as tutorial expertise could not be expected to cope with everything from the subtleties of ballet to the intricacies of film-making. Said the College sternly: 'it depends on the quality of the student'. Occasionally, then, one or other activity was a trifle trivial or half-baked. The other difficulty was the converse of this – the task of following up so diverse a range of activities without which, as one teacher wrote, 'it could merely be a pleasant diversion, with no lasting benefit to the children'. It was, therefore, necessary to limit the options for both these reasons; equally, just as students must master his or her leisure pursuit completely, it is essential for teachers to demonstrate a little more invention in terms of continuation programmes.

5. Junior creative expression

The aim was to begin with a stimulus of a local or relevant nature, leading to a spectrum of creative expression, via language, art, craft, music, drama and movement. All kinds of outlets, from modelling, sculpture and imaginative writing to instrumental music and tape-recordings, were deployed. This attempt 'to trigger off' children in these varied kinds of imaginative communication rested on the hypothesis that a growing awareness of the environment and an articulate response to it could be strengthened by a broad gamut of opportunity. Children blocked in one avenue of expression (say, language) could find a way through another avenue (say, movement). This mini-project moved away from the conventions of progressive creativity in schools by its insistence on a social priority. But, in scope of methods and an acceptance of first-hand experience as crucial, it was an exemplary illustration of the genre.

Normally, a term was set aside for a particular theme and the children grouped in sixes under the guidance of a student. One group took 'buildings' and 'our streets' as its termly offering: the other took 'space' (in the immediate environment, as well as its cosmic manifestation), 'Liverpool' and, like the twin group, 'our streets'. Some of the structuring was ingenious. With 'space', each group was named after a planet, and 'satellites' were awarded in lieu of group merit points. The stimuli were injected variously. For instance, with 'buildings', a whole series of visits, by group and class, were arranged to representative or notable buildings in the area, and these provoked an enormous amount of response. One 'space' exploration began with the question 'have we sufficient space in our classroom?', and eventually led to productions as ostensibly unconnected as a model solar system and a model of the school.

The material produced was of a high order, both in amount and inventiveness. Apart from some fine visual effects, like a model of the new Metropolitan Cathedral and a splendid mock-up stained-glass window, some of the concerted items were excellent. One thinks of 'Liverpolitania', an amusing set of mimes and movement patterns, with some choral support, on city life, or a mini-opera, 'Our Streets', composed and performed by the children.

To the project team, outside looking in, the atmosphere in which this exploration was conducted and the clear evidence of happy and excellent productivity, growing weekly before our eyes, was most encouraging. The work demonstrated that, from a base of the locality and its problems, the possibilities for creative expression are endless. Many teachers, of course, are aware of this, but there are still lingering and nostalgic beliefs in the efficacy of rather more ethereal and avowedly aesthetic stimuli. Moreover, the acceptance of a 'social' element in creativity is much less marked and, one might hope, this exercise could indicate to others that both immediacy and social purpose can be prime parts of creative experience.

6. Junior animal plant-life

This project was initiated in a school with a tradition of interest in animals and plants. The fact that one classteacher was most concerned obviously led to some emphasis for her own class, but the whole school had the chance to benefit from this enterprise. The background for the work was an animal room which increasingly became well-stocked. Its central figure, a veritable project mascot, was Pepi the parrot, who, to everyone's sorrow, was stolen partway through the project. Several budgerigars were also stolen, although this had a brighter side in that parents rallied round to replace them. The good Orangewoman who provided the replacements did so on condition that the one previously called Paddy should be substituted by one called Billy. This underlined the risk of animal-care, with its danger of great disappointment to children when creatures are harmed or stolen. In this case there was no wanton behaviour as such; merely the theft of marketable birds and a strict ignoring of the other animals, such as rabbits, guinea pigs, fish, hamsters and mice.

The intensification of the work from this base was critical, for it is precisely in the city school that animal-plant facilities are at a discount, so that extreme measures, like the equipping of large animal rooms and relatively distant excursions, is necessary. Another dimension was also added by way of a look at the possibilities for home engagement in animal and plant rearing. The children in this school were mainly drawn from highrise dwellings, where the ordinary run of gardens and pets are severely limited. One had to turn to the cultivation of faintly exotic seeds, like orange and lemon pips, to the planting of bulbs and the nurture of insect life, such as butterfly larvae. This was done by

D

giving a group of children the chance to take home some such smallscale experiment and by following this up by periodic appraisals of growth and development. This can hardly take the place of the puppy or the flower bed and, indeed, it is perhaps a criticism of highrise development that children are denied these pleasures. However, the balance of a well-fitted animal and plant-life set-up in the school, plus the encouragement of home activities, seemed acceptable enough and certainly led to some delightful work.

The whole question of 'rural' activity in 'urban' areas is a moot one. Should one in school endeavour to feed in this kind of experience, precisely because it is slightly unreal and not much open for children to pursue, or should one concentrate on, say, tinkering with motor cars and other urban phenomena? The stimulation afforded children especially by animals (less so by bulbs and so on which are somewhat tedious and lethargic in their growth) prompts one to suggest that the domestication of animals, frequently the province of the conventional home, might need to be adopted by the EPA schools, whose multilet and highrise catchments militate against this. Many schools, of course, do just this and for all sorts of valid reasons, such as biology and zoology. What is being emphasized here is the sheer social, homelike need for pets and, whereas schools have rightly concentrated on less likely animals (guinea pigs, for example), there may well be some reason, where circumstances permit, to introduce the notably urban dog-cat type of pet. Whatever else, the emphasis should rest (as in this school) on the everyday possibilities and requirements of the children, supported by external visits and excursions, as opposed to the almost subconsciously jeering dangling of improbable vistas of animals and flowers before city children, without doing anything to enliven their constant existence with these things.

A cheerful example of the 'multiplier effect' was provided by this animal room, for its inmates sturdily supported the project by their fecundity. Other project schools were able to receive rabbits and guinea pigs and mice from this source and, eventually, there was the charming development of cross-mating between animals from different schools. All in all, the animal project was a most lively affair, with the children finding huge enjoyment in the work, and opening out their other curricular activities from this base in an excellent manner.

It was in this school that the student-team branched out more than most others into the mainstream of school-life and became a sort of task-force for the entire school. This was a random team of differing subject specialists, who, apart from their assistance in the animal and plant studies, were used right throughout the school in all types of ways. One splendid instance of this was the 'junk' sculpture which one of the students developed with the children, a fine example of using the immediate environment for creative purposes. A fish, made from an old motor-bike petrol tank, and a warrior, with a bicycle wheel shield, were but two of a collection which drew widespread comment.

7. Infant social and creative studies

In the opening year, visits and other external stimuli were used to awaken children's curiosity in their environment and as a focus for some most cheerful and colourful work. From this base a more programmed approach was planned for the second year, when a full series of 'festivals' was adopted as the foci for most aspects of circular work. There can be little doubt that the results were vivid and unusually attractive. From Hallow'een, Harvest Festival via Guy Fawkes, Christmas, Pancake Tuesday and so on, right through to Spring and Easter, this serial held up extraordinarily well, with an everfresh complex of varied activities. One of the pleasantest touches was the emphasis on cookery related to the event. Around the Hallow'een period the production of the famous Everton Toffee, with a role-playing of the locally legendary character, Mother Noblett of the Everton Toffee-shop, was an instance of this.

The school believed that basic skills improved because of the interest aroused in the preparation and celebration of the festivals and special mention was made of improved language. The attached college agreed that the enterprise was successful and commented on the way students gained from seeing 'demands made and met by staff'. In general, the use of a set of reality-based themes, like the recurrent and popular festivals, was highly productive and seemed not to inhibit any of the conventional infant needs. Without any strain, all the strands of infant work –

number, music, drama, language, movement, creativity – fell readily into the pattern.

A major element in this project was the use of the actual festival for parental participation. The class engaged in the particular festival invited their parents to witness the previous weeks' activities as they blossomed to fruition on the appointed date. This was, according to the school 'very successful'. Parents enjoyed this pleasant way of seeing and tasting their children's work. This is the right atmosphere in which to coax the shy parent to relax and have fun, and at the same time these sessions are informative. The college said that these 'parent contacts in school with students is worth many lectures'. All in all, this was one of the project's best illustrations of combined curricular-parental activity, so much so that, in recording it, it has been pleasingly difficult to differentiate between home/school links and the curriculum. Maybe our goal should be the end of that distinction.

I have no doubt that social education can be as intellectually invigorating and emotionally rewarding as material arbitrarily labelled 'academic'. Similarly, I have been unmoved by critics who complain that a constant 'social' diet would be boring. I have never been happy with educational content justified purely as 'interesting'. Interest is, of course, vital, but it is the method used which should make material interesting rather than a soft-centred reliance on the material itself. Social purpose, not interest, should be the yardstick for the curriculum; interest is the criterion by which the chosen method should be judged. As for all those other 'skills' which people tell us children need, if they are so essential in life, why are not life-themes more frequently used to exercise them?

We have seen in the Liverpool schools hints of the possibilities of community-oriented curricula, principally dwelling on the familiarization of the child with his own society in all its flavours and moods. Where schools reject this need, preferring (sometimes on 'compensatory' grounds) to cosset the children with the consolations of suburban culture, there is a danger. In offering an alien clime for an hour or so a day, it risks producing socially schizophrenic children. When this approach is added to a system where only a few are winning the educational prizes, then it is frustrating as well.

Social education consists largely of the exercise of social skills on related social materials. Because it invites the teacher to lead children in a critical investigation of the issues facing children and parents in city centres today, it implies that openendedness and toleration should be the finest hallmarks of effective teaching. This change of attitude, from the teacher as mentor in prejudged standards to the teacher as guide in the art of social choice and discrimination, is liable to throw some strain on the profession. It may well be the major obstacle to complete community schooling, for there are immense pressures on teachers to act as guardians rather than critics of the social scene.

Curricula reappraisal is arduous work, and, frankly, we would claim no more for our efforts than that they were encouraging. There were certainly no negative or damaging effects, like deterioration in traditional skills; indeed, most reports spoke of uplift in language and communications patterns. Many teachers involved in the Project aver that there is an extra stimulus and dimension to be found in environment-based studies. We are encouraged enough to believe that, if, at least, no harm accrues, it is worthwhile importing socially relevant materials into the curriculum, in the hope that, overall, social awareness and purpose might be generated. One common and welcome reaction was the integrational fluidity resulting from the exploration of these social themes, and this, again, was very heartening. Whatever the point of entry, most of these thematic approaches gave rise naturally to overflow into other curricular realms.

My own impression is that the time has come to ask schools to devote much more time to the social environment and that, in the Liverpool work, many pointers in this direction were given. Perhaps one could invite schools to spend, as a next stage in the transition to full-run community education, half their time on social environmental education. One bids so ambitiously because the need is so urgent, because the social or communal centre of interest can be embracing of all other curricular forms, and because it can enliven them all – the reading, the talking, the number, the art and so forth – in its process of relevant and immediate utility.

Certainly few of us working in these areas doubt the capacity of young children to undertake such studies, and I am convinced that, in the past, the social and creative potential of the urban child has been sadly underrated. The resilience and aplomb of these children is quite remarkable; maybe their social sharpness is, tragically, the consequence of the appalling responsibilities and problems that are thrust upon them. Nonetheless, that *is* the potential, and it should be accordingly tapped.

On the teaching side, the greatest practical difficulty is lack of apposite materials. If schools are to differ according to the communities they serve, then, obviously, curriculum resources must vary as well. It could, in fact, be argued that suppliers and publishers, who needs must sell their wares in Sunderland as well as Plymouth, contribute to the perpetuation of neuter, abstract and 'national' teaching in our schools. We produced five teaching kits, called 'Projectors', as examples of what was needed. Two of them, 'Streets Ahead', an urban social problems game, and 'Wotever Next?', a pre-school language kit, are still available. But the main progress was made with Liverpool's decision to develop a curriculum resources workshop for EPA teachers, where precisely the kind of materials required by the teachers could be created. This is the basis for a solution to the question, so often raised by teachers, of obtaining the requisite materials, and one would hope many other local authorities would follow this splendid Liverpool lead.

It is a lengthy and perhaps unending haul, but some of the omens are good. Progressive primary approaches, especially methods of controlled enquiry and the belief that children must learn from firsthand experience – are highly effective for social education purposes. The two combined and carried logically forward lead ineluctably to those forms of openended social investigation that are, or should be, the crux of the Community School curriculum. We felt, during the Project, that we were further opening doors on relevant content. Teachers will frequently say that the social environment is fine, but let's not forget the 'bread and butter' subjects. It is our ambition to make the social environment *the* 'bread and butter' subject.

School and community relations

As well as the curricular exploration, we experimented in the opening year with a variety of home and community projects. Some 15 or 20 had been floated; several of them came to naught; several looked likely, but were slow to mature; four came quickly to fruition. A consensus of empirical opinion (teacher, tutor, student, parent, child, ourselves, other interested parties) suggested that these had been successful.

The first of this quartet was the class coffee morning, during which parents and other relatives visited the classroom, partook of refreshments and watched or joined the children's work. We saw this as preparatory to parent-child projects, whereby the parent could see and contribute to the educational process. The class was deemed to be a better focus than the school for this kind of gathering and, pioneered by Windsor Street Junior School, this activity had an impressive beginning. The coffee mornings were well-attended and the parents professed much interest. Simply, parents cannot help unless they understand and the best way for them to learn is, so to speak, on the shop floor. Parents so often see only the end-product of education, when the child takes home his blotter or his model. For full understanding, it is necessary to observe, even better engage in, the blood, toil, sweat and tears of the actual process.

The second was the landscaping of the school playground for the benefit of the children and of the surrounding community. The garden devised for St Margaret's naturally needed much more time to mature, but the superb wall-murals painted on their playground walls by Chatsworth School juniors and infants made an immediate visual impact. They included a dramatic waterfront scene and they were decorated with hanging baskets and large bowls of flowers. This attractive ensemble quickly became a 'tourist' spot for visitors to the project and our fears of vandalism proved absolutely groundless, perhaps because the children and others felt it was part of themselves and invested considerable pride in the work. Both these schemes showed the happy coupling of curriculum and community themes in the project.

The third was home and school communication. We helped

publish a once-off prospectus for Chatsworth School, a high-class, well-illustrated description of the life and work of the school; the first of a series of well-presented school newsletters with articles on the work of the school, including one on ITA complete with a transcribed piece from the *Liverpool Echo* for parents to try out; and the first 'Solly', the magazine of the Salisbury School, a colourful anthology mainly of children's work, with articles from parents promised for the next edition. These were enormously well-received. They were followed up by questionnaires and most parents responded with enthusiasm; indeed, in the case of the first 'Solly', there was a 100% response to the questionnaire the following day! Each, in its way, was aimed at informing the homes of the aims and methods of the school, so that parents through enlarged comprehension might the better help their children. The important extra element was the professional nature of the publications – the prospectus was admirably glossy; the newsletter a remarkably skilled attempt to match the modes of the popular with the concern of the serious press and the magazine was delightful and pleasing to evoke a fine response from the parents of the school. In an age of expert mass media, the school must compete in line, for the day of the hurriedly duplicated note which finds its way to the back of the mantelpiece is surely doomed. We felt strongly that the teacher potential and the parent potential was there and that a more efficient machinery of communication must be constructed for them. The parents and teachers and, not least, children of EPAs are important enough to warrant the finest forms of communication available. One of the urgent EPA needs is public relations and this, it was felt, was a probable answer.

The fourth was the exhibition of schoolwork at that natural focal point of school and community, the shop. Salisbury School was instrumental in implementing this experiment. It began gingerly in one or two shops, but it sparked off an extension to a dozen or more shops adjacent to the school. Anywhere where people foregather is fair game for the presentation of schoolwork and for descriptions of educational processes. It gave talking-points as well as information to the community and they responded richly. The use of shops spread to other schools and, gradually, other meeting-points – the doctor's surgery, the pubs, the bingo hall, the factory canteen, and elsewhere – were utilized.

The home and school and community and school mini-projects were extended to other schools, and by the end of the second year they were in excellent shape. They were perhaps the most outward and visible signs of the Project, attracting a good deal of outside attention and publicity. As we progressed, the concept of school and home relations became more cleancut. To begin with, we soon dropped any formal differentiation between home and community probes for it became a valueless distinction. We had started by calling coffee mornings 'parental' and shop exhibitions 'communal', but, at base, there was no definitive difference. All our attempts in this field, then, we grouped together as lines of communication between the school and its social context.

And, through the actual operation of school-home links in the first year, we also began to see the problem more lucidly in such educational terms as the interacting effect of neighbourhood and school on the child. We began to talk of 'complementary', rather than 'compensatory' education, with the school endeavouring to establish rapport with the values of home and community, rather than, if only by implication, opposing them. The task, we felt more and more, was not so much to soup up the schools to make-good purported neighbourhood and family deficiencies; rather was it to create smoother relations with the parents and others in the community. The lesson of the suburban school is that it identifies with its environs.

The national survey of parental attitudes conducted by all the EPA teams confirmed much of what the successes of our home-school schemes suggested. Most parents are very much concerned about their children's schooling, especially in terms of its effect on job chances and so on. Moreover, they have, normally, a high regard for the professional teacher, whose task of looking after thirty or more children all day they rarely envy and often applaud. But their own educational shortcomings, which they are quick to recognize, and the strenuous pressure of everyday city life make it difficult for them to help their children and support the schools in what they are attempting. They had perhaps found schools off-putting and incomprehensible as children; the very changes in method we have rightly welcomed in our schools confuse the issue even more, so that parents frequently doubt the wisdom of intervention. Yet the goodwill exists, and, possibly more than anything else, I would claim for the EPA Projects that they have helped exorcize that persistent hobgoblin of educational demonology – the feckless, apathetic working-class parent.

The concern of these parents and their confidence in teaching staffs, which make some of our suburban parents look egocentric and hysterical, is a pleasing feature, and it has enormous potential. On the school side, many teachers seem to me now to be convinced of the vital necessity for strong and supportive home relationships. It must be said, over and over again, that parental links are not, at least in the short run, about teaching auxiliaries, or fund-raising PTAs or parent-power. The justification is initially educational. The aim is to augment the educational understanding of the parents and the social understanding of the teacher, so that a closer partnership for the education of the children might be realized. We have, I think, demonstrated the fine potential of both sides of the equation. It is a question of communication; of, if you like, public relations. Some of the mechanisms, the spare resources and energy (which only improved staffing would bring) and, inevitably, the correct training have thus far been lacking.

Our explorations have thrown up a series of techniques for attracting the interest of parents and others in the community. They suggest a logical process for involving the parent, moving from the indirect approach of the publication, via the site-improvement or exposition approaches, to the direct approach of the class focus and the parent-child project. There are no blanket answers. The teacher must assess the situation critically, taking into account the climate and character of the school, the mood and feelings of the parents, and, most crucially, his or her own temperament and personality. Then the choice must be made as to where broadly to join the sequence and which particular type of approach to use. It is a process which, hopefully, sees the parent move from observer to participant, from merely noting with interest what the school is attempting, to a more whole-hearted involvement with the actual work of the children. In this sense, the parent is in a learner-role, especially in the early phases of development; and there was nothing more significant in our work than this involvement of parents in the *process* of education, in addition to their normal part which is to view its end-product.

Windsor Street Juniors, in fact, experimented with such a project, running over four consecutive Tuesday evenings. The children of one class of 28 and their parents, aimed at producing a fifteen minute tape on the street as well as other kinds of work. Music-making, creative writing, reminiscence and dramatization of street scenes were included. This was hard work with two or three other teachers helping the class-teacher with aspects of the production and refreshments. The numbers were high the first week with twenty-seven children and thirty-five adults attending, but this was partially helped by a local car-worker strike which enabled some shift-working fathers to attend. Football matches affected attendance on the following two evenings, but, on the last night, numbers jumped again and the whole sequence ended satisfactorily. June Price, the class-teacher and a founder member of the project's Teacher Liaison Committee supervised the operation, and, as part of a most assiduous exercise, she completed a full series of home visits before and during the work. As one mother said, 'it's better than television'.

Extension was the critical point. The four major categories – parental at-homes, site improvement, publication and exhibition – were on offer in the second year to all the project schools. This was a significant test for the project. It was relatively easy to persuade a school to indulge in a short-term mini-scale experiment. It was of a different order when each of these schools was asked whether it wished (on top of its initial experimental tasks) to take on others. By now the project personnel at all levels was a compact and freely communicating group. There were regular meetings of the Head Teachers' Standing Committee and the Teachers' Liaison Committee. The practice of exchanging visits developed spontaneously and many teachers commented on this being, in itself, an important breakaway from the isolation of much school teaching. Teachers, therefore, attended coffee mornings at Windsor Street, inspected the wall-murals at Chatsworth, and interchanged school publications. They were able to see and discuss how it was done and raise possible pitfalls with the pioneer schools. In the main, they were impressed by the compelling nature of the wall-murals and the interest they adduced both in children and others, in the professional lay-out of the school publications (by now 'Solly' included parents' items) and in the enthusiastic response to them, and in the unquestionably eager and large groupings which attended coffee mornings without any apparent disruption. About this time, a further short BBC 1 (North) Television item on coffee mornings helped press the cause. The teacher interviewed, when asked whether children or parents benefited most, suggested that it was, in fact, the teacher who gained as much as either. Others interviewed pointed to instances of their own improved grasp of school aims and the introduction of school techniques (art materials, for instance) into the home situation.

Given the hardheaded and cautious investigation by the headteachers and staffs, the results of 'multiplication' were encouraging. For instance, the first school to attempt wall-murals had not rested content, but was forging ahead to the extent that, having painted the inside of every wall, the teachers and children were threatening to start on the outside. They had added indoor scenes as well as an animal scene (Infant) and a physical-education scene (Junior) and, as in all this work, the preparatory discussions, scaling and modelling were an intrinsic part of the teaching exercise. In brief, the walls became a natural place to set out and develop normal curriculum work. Most compelling of all was a huge football scene some eighty feet long by fifteen feet high. It had a full-size goal – functional, for the children to shoot in – all the trappings of stands, adverts, markings, players – diplomatically divided between the red of Liverpool and the royal blue of Everton – and, nicest of all, each junior child painted a face in the crowd. It really was a most striking achievement. And, as one six year old said while painting away at the animal scene, to Brian Jackson, the Director of ACE, 'I suppose when we've finished this, the television will come again'. This school, which had already produced the model prospectus for the project and itself, also found time to begin coffee mornings as well. Two other schools had adopted the coffee morning ploy and interesting variations began to emerge, like spreading the class about the school on varied activities and escorting the parents to the different groups, or a quiet restaurant-like room set aside for coffee and talk with small groups of parents moving into the actual classroom-situation periodically.

The school, where site improvement meant reclamation of a large patch of derelict ground for a garden, stolidly proceeded with its arduous plan, by this time with some student aid. Obviously, reclaiming land was considerably more laborious than painting walls, but, with judicious planting and paving and the deployment of a bench here and a shrub there, the metamorphosis slowly took place. And, for good measure, indoor and outdoor murals were tried to relieve the drabness of dull walls. Again with student help, a school magazine-cum-newsletter was started. This school was also the location for the Tuesday Club, an informal mothers' group begun by Trilby Shaw, the assistant action-research officer. For the eleven project school departments which had started some and accepted other ventures, the count at the end of the second year read: site improvement schemes six; direct parental link-ups of the coffee morning type – seven; professional devised publications, school to home, produced or planned – twelve; (one school attempting two varieties). Six schools were also attempting to involve parents with varying degrees of success in the normal round of school outings to local zoos, beauty spots, school camps, and so on. Twenty-five efforts were gratifying. What was of further gratification was the refusal slavishly to follow a party-line; this partly was due to a sterling denial of just copying someone else blindly, and partly due to the shrewd adaptation of a tactic to the circumstances and dictation of each especial situation. The variegation of publications, with school calendars vying with curriculum-oriented booklets, was a typical illustration, the underlying common denominator being their polished professional presentation. The modification of playground wall-murals to the indoors or to suit functional purposes, like target practice or football games is another instance. Similarly, attempts to draw in parents on a regular basis were extremely varied, but all of them aimed at giving the parent a chance to view and understand the educative process.

The home/school relations programme continued into the

third year with practically every one of the thirty or so schools attempting to meet this critical need. Something like twenty schools were now organizing direct contacts at parental at-homes and their like, and all the schools were reporting back to the project team of the success of their efforts and the high degree to which they intended to make such enterprises a permanent aspect of the school's life. There were now several school publications going the rounds, but printing costs were on the increase and so were the numbers of schools. It was impossible to publish individually, nor did all schools feel they had the time or energy to trouble themselves with such a production. We hit upon the idea of 'Back Home', a four-sided journal for parents (see pp. 111–14 for an example of the journal), of which about 10,000 were distributed through the schools once a term. It was edited in a stylish and pleasantly conversational manner by Trilby Shaw, and its readable contents touched on items of interest to parents – the teaching of reading, coffee mornings and so forth. For each of the three editions, a main theme – home and school, curriculum and the community, school and community – was developed, and the schools reported favourably on the impression 'Back Home' made. The major point about 'Back Home' was that it could be used independently or as a stout cover for the school, class or individual material. Some schools duplicated quite large magazines with illustrations and other trimmings which stapled neatly inside 'Back Home'. In this way, it resembled the Football League Review or the Church Magazine (depending where one spent one's week-ends), in its combine of general and particular coverage. Others used it to sugar the pill of forms and other documents that had to be dispatched to the home, while others used it as a cover for the carol service or school entertainment programme. The schools tended to find it of some value and only one out of thirty-four schools refused to distribute it. Some schools regarded it as an excellent addition to the project's stock in trade.

During the year, we began to develop the idea of the Education Kiosk, along the lines of the normal education shop but visualized as a packable mobile kit. It was composed of a freestanding three-part screen, with racks for literature, copies of twenty-three single-sheet leaflets especially prepared on all aspects of edu-

Back home

Issue 3   Published by E P A Project
Paddington Comprehensive School
Liverpool L73EA telephone 709 2273

LOOK OUT! THE SCHOOL IS MOVING . . .
Moving out, that is, into the community

it serves and which keeps the school going; moving out to tell the parents and other people who live near the school what the teachers and children are attempting to do.

Back home, they'll be watching and
   waiting and cheering every move
Back home tho' they think we're the
   greatest, that's what we've got
   to prove.
We'll be put to the test, knowing
   we'll give all we've got to give.
For the folks back home!

There's 'Back Home' for a start . . .

Most journals boast about their circulation, so why shouldn't we? We publish 12,000 copies and the children take it home (at least, we *hope* they take it home) from thirty-four schools. This is one way of taking the school into the community. But what has really surprised us has been the way schools like St. Alexander's Juniors have used *Back Home* as we intended to use it; they use it as a cover for their own neat, attractive and interesting magazine or newsletter. We're building up quite a collection of clever ways in which schools have sent out their own local material to the parents with the help of *Back Home*.

. . . and the others

Some city schools have their own publication. These are very exciting and varied. There's *Solly*, the colourful magazine of Salisbury Primary School; *Bewey Board Bulletin*, the splendid Beaufort St. School Journal, *News and views*, the highly informative newspaper from St. Francis Xavier's Boys, the fascinating St. Margaret's School Magazine, the splendid Windsor Infants calendar, and others.

All of them attempt to let you, the mothers and fathers, know what's happening, so that your interest can be that much more informed. And, of course, it's nice for the children to see their work and their friend's work in print.

IT'S A NEW LOOK AT GEOGRAPHY

We've moved from the old Geography of Arctic and Antarctic to the new Geography of Street and Shop. These are the things which form the child's real environment. These are the real base of his education.

COCKING A SNOOK at their sometimes drab environment is a marvellous way for children to show the outside world they're ready to have a go at improving matters. Several schools have very impressive murals on their playground walls, all of them developing out of work in the school, and all of them a fine sight for passers-by. Chatsworth School, both junior and infant, first began this move and now the entire playground walls are covered with huge, dramatic scenes of the jungle, the Liverpool waterfront, a gym lesson and a football match. St. Margaret's have reclaimed a fairsized part of their site, which had become derelict, and transformed it into a school garden. St. Francis Xavier Boys have used their roof playground both for murals *and* garden. We reckon there are now 16 schools trying these site-improvement schemes.

SHOPPING FOR SCHOOL is another way into the life of the community. Everyone goes to the shops, so the schools must be there to greet them. Exhibitions of work in shops have proved very popular and sometimes the idea spreads very quickly. Salisbury School, exhibiting in the Soho St. area of West Everton, had a weekly change of exhibits at a dozen shops, with a doctor's surgery and a couple of pubs thrown in for good measure. Have you been down Lodge Lane recently? Tiber St. Infants have some really remarkable products on view in the shops down there. It doesn't have to be shops—factories, bingo halls, community centres, railway stations, church halls—anywhere that people gather is a place for the school to be busy.

Setting up the Happy Circle

The more the children investigate their environment, writing, talking, painting, and modelling about it, and the more what they produce is on show to the parents and others in the community, the more harmonious is the whole business. For instance, a child takes a look at his local street; he writes a poem about it; the poem goes in the school magazine which goes out to the people in the street or on exhibition in a local shop on that street; the circle is complete. Even better, one or two schools, such as St. Margaret's and Windsor Juniors, have had a go at getting the parents and children to work together on projects about the street, its characters and its character. When parents do the work alongside their own children, they can really begin to appreciate what it's all about; and then they can help their children profitably. So keep the circle complete. It's bad luck to break the circle!

WHAT ABOUT MOVING TO SECONDARY SCHOOL?

Ken Vaux
HEADMASTER, PADDINGTON
COMPREHENSIVE SCHOOL

Do you know your son or daughter?

Of course you do. You have known him or her all his or her life. You knew him when he was a baby. Perhaps you still think of him as a baby. He is beginning to think of himself as a man. Truth is somewhere between your view and his. Is he ready to change to a Secondary School?

The calendar can lie

If he reaches the age of eleven between the 2nd of September 1970 and the 1st of September 1971 he will be transferred to a Secondary School on the 1st of September 1971. Children mature at different rates. Some need help to prepare them for the changeover.

What are the differences between Secondary and Primary Schools?

Size. Most Secondary Schools are much bigger than Primary Schools. There is much more movement. The pupils are expected to know where to go without being told. Control is looser. Opportunities for making mistakes are more numerous. The pupils are bigger and the oldest are young men and women.

How can a parent help in preparation?

This depends on many things. The most common need of an eleven year old child is for greater self reliance. Can he cook a meal? Would you send him to Manchester alone?

Can he wash and iron a shirt? Can he go to a restaurant and get a meal? Do you talk to him as if he were an adult? Try just for one day to speak to him without giving an order, a reprimand or a piece of advice. It is very difficult but necessary if he is to begin disciplining himself, and in a Secondary School he should be moving steadily towards self-discipline. There will be discipline in his new school if he still needs strict control when he leaves the Secondary School then he has not been properly educated.

Can I help in the choice of Secondary School?

In Liverpool parents are allowed to name five schools in order of preference. A list of available schools can be seen either at your child's Primary School or at the Education Office at 14 Sir Thomas Street.

If you ask for a place in a selective school your child's ability will be taken into account. If you ask for a place in a Comprehensive School or a Secondary the places will be awarded according to your address. Places are first given to those living nearest.

The first person to see is your child's Primary School Headteacher who will give you an assessment of his potential and may recommend a Secondary School.

It is also useful to try to see one or more Secondary Schools. Many schools have open days or similar occasions when members of the public are welcome. At some schools it is possible to have an interview with the Head or a Senior member of staff. Such an interview can do no harm and may be very helpful. Write to the Headteachers of several schools asking what facilities are offered for parents to see the school. The answers themselves should assist you. Some schools provide brochures or pamphlets setting out the courses available in the school. These too will assist you.

How can I be sure that he will be happy in his new school?

You can't. Unless he is seriously maladjusted he should quickly adapt himself. If you are anxious, keep your anxieties to yourself. If you and your wife argue about him, do it after he has gone to bed. Treat his change of school as something exciting but not a matter for doubts and fears. Be interested but don't fuss. Children are rarely communicative about school and cross-examinations about school are not helpful to parent or child. If you are anxious about him write to the Head but avoid criticism of the school until you have heard other accounts besides his.

Being Prepared

He will probably need a new uniform, overalls and kit for games and P.E. He can be helped if your income is limited, both by a uniform grant and by provision of school meals. Apply in good time. Forms can be obtained from any school or from the Education Office. If he travels more than two and a half miles to school he will be given a travel contract.

The Timid Child

You feel that he will be bullied in his new school. He is shy, withdrawn, lonely. You want to protect him. All mothers and some fathers feel like this. Remember that you cannot change the world to suit him. It is very difficult to change him to suit the world. The only thing you can change is any attitudes of your own which may have made him what he is. Nagging is easy and of little value. Example is much harder but much more effective. Your quiet confidence can be catching. Your fears are also catching. So is class consciousness. Do not grade schools by the social class they serve. It is not so important as most parents think. No Secondary School will give a cosy cocoon nor would such an environment be good for a child.

Can I help my son with his work?

It is most unlikely that he will welcome help with homework or schoolwork. Encourage him to read. Not only by giving him good books but by drawing his attention to an interesting article in the *Echo*. You can fill in the gaps that school leaves. Show him your income tax form; your friendly society pass book; your insurance policies; your union card; house repairs. Perhaps out of such discussions you may find what his ambitions are. In discussing careers be generous with information and niggardly with advice.

The last word

Schools are not run by supermen for idiots; nor are they run by idiots for supermen. They are like other institutions, good in parts. Nevertheless the modern Secondary School offers wonderful opportunities and a variety unknown in the past. Your child will enjoy himself.

WE HOPE YOU WILL FIND THIS GOOD NEWS

It's likely that *Back Home*, having completed its third pioneer edition of the year, will be back next year with issues at Christmas, Easter and Summer cation, both curricular (e.g. modern maths, reading, etc.) and administrative (e.g. parental choice, zoning, special education, etc.) and a uniform for the assistant. The colours and pattern of the kiosk, literature and uniform were constant, making for a unified kit which could quickly be erected at any focal point, be it bingo hall, railway station, factory canteen, department store or football ground. In the summer of 1971, this was used experimentally with many signs of overall interest, at the Liverpool Show which commands an audience of thousands over its three-day duration. It is hoped that this device might be produced on a larger scale in the coming years. There is an obvious need to get educational information quickly and simply to the population, and it must be done at a wide gamut of vantage points, moving out to people the opportunity of raising queries, rather than waiting quietly for the clients to find the information service. A self-evident corollary of this is the need to offer an attractive, self-contained presentation and to ensure the kiosk attendants are rigorously trained to meet questions tidily and sympathetically.

Probably the most encouraging omen in the home/school field was the growing inability to decide when an activity was a home/school link, or a piece of curricular development. The child-parent projects on the street themes are neat illustrations; they were efforts both to find an environmental way into the curriculum and to engage parental interest. It is when it is difficult to decide between one formal category and the other, that community schooling is really beginning to buzz. One could see signs of community-school 'circles' or 'cycles' evolving. One of these – at St Margaret's School – was deftly illustrated on a Granada Television programme. It showed the children working in Faulkner Square with our 'Down Our Way' workbook – this was a 'Projector' example, developed by Frank Harris, a curriculum adviser to the project, and one which proved very popular – and reading poetry they had written as a result of their investigations; then the poems were included in the school magazine which went back out on the streets to the local community. Against the backcloth of a reclaimed school garden, a Mothers' Club discussing abortion and shots of the school's wall-murals, this spiral effect was well-demonstrated. The circular nature of community schooling was growing ever more evident now, with 'ventures out' sustaining 'welcomes in' and vice versa.

Nor were the teachers forgotten. Our three liaison committees – heads, tutors and teachers – continued to meet, enjoying the expansive catering of Paddington's Home Management Department and feeling, it was said, that there was much benefit to be gained in themselves from such friendly and informative encounters. The social scene, which had begun modestly enough with a peaceful sherry party, gradually developed. This reached something of a riotous climax with an olde tyme music hall at Paddington, attended by about a hundred teachers. The project staff performed and stewarded, with the help of the Paddington Band, the Paddington Staff and, once more, the Home Management Department with a menu of Edwardian splendour. Suffice it to say that it became almost impossible to halt the proceedings.

Adult education

By the end of year two, Tom Lovett, our WEA tutor-organizer attached, had completed his first year of exploration of adult educational problems in the EPA. It was an awesome task which he attacked with commendable fortitude and resource. Whereas the project proper had seven nominated schools and the preschool campaign had a nucleus of a score or more playgroups, adult education had no obvious core. There was a huge population of 100,000 with a complicated pattern of activities hither and thither. The issue had two sides, content and method. Adult education for the working-class, it appeared, was failing on both sides, with neither the type of syllabus nor the type of course structure seemingly popular. The only compensation was the fact that the project had already made some contacts at adult level, notably through school-parental links, and these were available for Tom Lovett to capitalize.

The first six months were occupied, predictably, by reconnaissance, but, true to the theme of the Liverpool project, it was a sounding out in action. Tom Lovett attempted a most varied collection of probes, again in line with the broadscale exploration of the project at large. As with the other aspects of the project, the danger was overstretching, a tendency to overcommit per-

sonnel and resources to so many features, that scarcely any could
be beneficially controlled. Thus, there was a determination to
alight on one or two favourable loci and undertake a thoroughgoing pilot scheme. After all, Tom Lovett's brief was similar at
adult level to the project's at the school level – to demonstrate in
action, as a future model, the success or failure of particular
educational ventures. It was not his job to solve the problem of
the entire area at one fell swoop.

This exploratory period is difficult to describe shortly, without
over-simplifying. Four main elements do, however, stand out.
First, there was the usual progression of visits and visitors as the
character and resources of the environment were opened up to
the WEA tutor, a phase watched sympathetically by older-ser-
ving members of the project team, for it is a frustrating phase. It
is, of course, essential, but so much in retrospect must be wasteful
and jettisoned. Second, there was the attempt to try schemes on
for size. Some of these were of the home and school variety,
endeavouring to find in what form and for what purpose groups
of parents might join together on educational grounds. There
were also experiments in connection with community centres,
one of which led, in turn, to a revealing short course for young
adults on love and marriage, conducted with three groups in a
Liverpool EPA neighbourhood centre, in a suburban youth club
and with a co-educational fifth form. There was a substantial
amount of work with the Shelter scheme (SNAP) within the
project area, including the organization of a 24-session course for
personnel for the SNAP Information Centre. Tom Lovett
became a leading member of the Educational Task Force, one of
a number of such groups appended to SNAP, in the desire for
fullscale communal participation in the Shelter rehabilitation
programme. Third, there was the urgent necessity to describe
and analyse the non-formal communal activity of the area. It was
patently evident that the existing format of schools, youth clubs,
community centres, churches and what have you, did not cater
for all social needs. It was equally evident that many might be
suspicious of or antagonistic towards the existing structure, and
that, for instance, a variegated mosaic of groupings might be
preferable for the local culture than the more normal large centre
or institution at salient locations. With voluntary and student

help, this exercise of describing and mapping the complete con-course of social activity in a given neighbourhood was set in train. If adult education was to occur naturally and spon-taneously, an intimate knowledge of social functions, be it bingo or boozing, was a pre-requisite. Fourth, it was important to work out some approximate theory or perspective of EPA adult edu-cation using, among other items, this social recreational sur-vey.

This working rule of thumb as it emerged was at one with the general philosophy of the project. It sought to discover growth-points of educational needs within the target population and to succour them by the discreet use of experts. It sought also to base the activity in an ongoing social situation, like a mothers' group or a youth club. The development of a 'course' as such was gradual, evolving slowly from the foregathering of people nat-urally and their coming to an awareness of an educational need. Simply, it was the exact opposite of the conventional decision to organize a course and, through advertisement, to tempt people to attend. It worked in reverse order, beginning with an existing group of people and the manifestation of need for some form of education. This is the adult equivalent of the Liverpool Project attitude to education in its call for an open-ended, relevant ap-proach with children and, by the same token, adults, who have not had the opportunity, helped to become profoundly aware of their community, its problems and the possible responses they can create to solve them. An enterprise like SNAP is a pointer to the difficulty whereby people are sincerely invited to participate in replanning their environs, who have never been educated to do so. In Tom Lovett's own words, 'this, then, throws a great burden on the adult educationist who must tackle the problem of those who have come through the system without benefiting greatly from it. If the EPA philosophy is a correct analysis of the problems, then adult education, far from being a continuous process, is one of fundamental remedial education for a sizeable proportion of the population. The adult educationalist is facing the same problems of the primary schoolteacher, but at a later stage, and thus, I would argue, has a great deal to learn from the methods and content of the EPA approach to primary edu-cation.'

As a consequence of this four-pronged examination of the situation, it was decided that the Salisbury Community Centre, West Everton, formed the likeliest focus for a relatively massive follow-up. Although it was not envisaged that all the eggs would go in the same basket and that all other connections would be severed, this was programmed for a major pilot investigation of adult educational needs. This centre was situated in old, un-tenanted LEA premises. These were, in fact, a handicraft centre, strategically placed between two EPA project schools and within a few yards of each. Father Woodhall (Chairman of the EPA PA Steering Committee) had been active in promoting this new usage and he was eager, as were others in the area both pro-fessional and lay, to utilize the building still further. The Sal-isbury Community Centre, as it came to be named, was ideally placed for adult educational, social and recreational activities. It lay in Salisbury Street at the centre of a large working-class, mainly highrise, locality; a playgroup under our auspices had given it the impetus of a start; and the project was already closely allied with it.

The premises had many internal advantages for this purpose, although, initially, these were austerely balanced by the dis-advantages of a faulty heating system, broken windows and inad-equate maintenance. A series of negotiations with the LEA and, with help of local councillors, began to bear fruit. These, not surprisingly, were protracted, for, in practice, the LEA was being invited to hand over a building lock, stock and barrel to a com-munity group, newly-formed, and yet continue to finance its maintenance and caretaking. Alternatively, and with equal good sense, the Salisbury people ached to lay their hands on a disused building when the need for it was so burning. Slowly, the tech-nical detail was surmounted, the building took on some form of workable shape and, under Tom Lovett's careful guidance, a community centre grew before our very eyes.

Its evolution followed the rough and ready theory already enunciated. In and around the playgroup, mothers met on a number of occasions and soon found themselves discussing the area's lack of social amenities. It was eventually suggested that the building might be deployed beyond the thrice-weekly play-group. This was greeted enthusiastically and, significantly, it led to increased turn-out at the next get-together and the following week over forty people assembled to debate the possibility of a community centre. A Committee was elected and, within four weeks, a boxing club was started, twice-weekly dances for teenagers were held, a jumble sale was arranged, hairdressing and keep-fit classes were begun, the local councillors were met face to face and the centre affiliated itself to the West Everton Community Council.

This occurred in an area where, cynics scoffed, people had lost the will and capacity for self-organization. Rather did it succeed precisely because it was the people's own initiative that mattered; they collected the boxing gear and provided the crockery; it was the group from down the street which provided the music for the dance. Even more pleasingly, from the EPA viewpoint, there was grave concern shown about the needs of youngsters. Much of the emphasis in discussion was on activities for children and youth. It demonstrated yet again the vital interest parents and others have in education and, at the Salisbury Centre, there was an encouraging desire to act accordingly.

By a process then of internal community combustion, sparked off and, to pursue an atrocious metaphor, revved up by Tom Lovett, a small-scale experiment in adult education was begun. It could be argued that the adults were educating themselves by doing, that most praised of primary school techniques. They had admitted responsibility for some of the social and educational problems of their neighbourhood and were intent on solving them. It was adult education in its broadest sense, and when, as it was hoped, something of a more formal nature was introduced, this would be no more than a cultivation of a healthy and organic growth. Indeed, in the September of 1970 it was decided to float rather more conventional courses, albeit with a strong social and communal content. Eventually, the centre was granted substantial Urban Aid support.

The next step was to programme activities over a lengthier time-span and in more detail. As well as sustaining the existing activities, it was planned to begin parental classes on educational matters, establish educative links with informal social groups as in pubs or clubs based on the survey of such amenities in the district, and provide similar services to local youth clubs and residents' associations.

Another adult field in which we dabbled was school management. We arranged a 3-session Course and provided trimmings such as delicious and gratis refreshments and invigorating and gratis reading matter. Our first confirmation of the myth of school managerial apathy was that, of the sixty-three invitations to the school managers of the project schools, less than twenty replied despite our forwarding of a printed pre-addressed, stamped postcard which required but a tick or two and a popping into the pillar box. An average of eleven managers attended the three meetings. The first was ably addressed by Tom McManners, the Liverpool Chief Inspector, on the actual powers of school managers. The second was a seminar on role analysis, fascinatingly led by Tom Ward of the John Moores Company. This produced several startling instances of clashes of role awareness, role fulfilment and the realities of the situation. The third was a mock school managers' meeting, pleasantly chaired by Pat Taylor, Chairman of the Granby managers. It was, at times, terrifyingly realistic, as disbelief was suspended and the managers worked with earnest will. It was notable for performances by Councillor Mrs Simey as a stone-walling 'mock' LEA officer and by Ken Vaux, Head of Paddington School who, as the 'mock' headteacher demonstrated how craftily headteachers could lead managers off the straight and narrow and into discussions engineered by the headmaster's report.

Despite low numbers it was an enjoyable and useful little course, much appreciated by course members and very instructive to the project team. The low attendance, plus the issues that emerged, certainly underlined the need for fairly substantial training programmes for managers. In terms of the Community School, school managers have an increasingly more important part to play as bridges or interpreters between school and community. Their job could be crucial. Two points, therefore, must be made. It is clear that school managers should be much more representative than now of the communities they affect to serve. Political has-beens and never-quites must make way for those who know the community and are prepared to serve effectively.

Many councillors do sterling work on management committees and, as local government experts and linksmen with the LEA, the Education Committee and the Council, they are invaluable. But it would seem sensible to ally them with those representing other related interests, such as the social community, the parents, the teaching staff and the local business world. Thereby would a consensus of view and action be more likely to emerge. A change in purpose is the concomitant of this change in structure. The task of the manager in the EPA Community School (if not else-where) needs to become less administrative and more social-cum-educative as he strives in a variety of directions to enhance the harmony between school and neighbourhood. He should be the person who explains the one to the other and constantly helps to draw them together.

During the 1970–71 session, the adult education programme built up to a peak of some score or more weekly groups, and the Salisbury Community Centre continued its excellent progress. There were many signs that Tom Lovett was engineering some-thing of a breakthrough in adult education, and he himself, en-couraged as always by David Connor, the WEA District Secretary, worked diligently both to cement the gains made, and also give maximum publicity to those novel methods in what has been somewhat of a limited field in the past. The business of dialogue in non-formal situations, exploring towards rather more structured course work, eventually, much of it of a social nature, was an arduous and tiring one. Perhaps the biggest barrier was the adult education regime, necessarily beset with rules about finance and registration. Assuredly, it was flexibility in these matters – and here the WEA proved more than willing to experi-ment – which proved most successful, and it is certain that such flexibility must become a major element in plans for adult edu-cation if inroads are to be made in working-class areas.

An especially exciting innovation was Tom Lovett's devising of six local radio scripts, complete with appropriate music, inter-view and dramatization. Radio Merseyside transmitted these under the title of 'Talk, Gentlemen, Please', and they formed a 'Living Today' series, dealing with the school, the church, local government, the family and so on. Considerable national interest was caused by this series, but an even more significant feature was the reception of these fifteen-minute programmes at a set of vantage points as the stimulus for tutor-led group discussion. No less than ten groups were established in pubs and community centres to hear and debate this weekly series. It was estimated that, on average, 120 adults attended these groups, apart from the normal reception of the programmes by other radio listeners. Careful logging of reactions was completed by the tutors in order to assess the possibilities of this type of attack. Local radio could play a crucial role in community development and localized democracy; Radio Merseyside had already demonstrated how local radio can pinpoint and meet the localized educational needs of children in some ways better than the national radio and television circuits; now it was set fair to offer the same service for adults. There was some hope as the series ended that a grant might be obtained for developing the style and content of adult education, via the medium of local radio. It was obviously a most fertile field.

A further adult venture was sponsored in conjunction with the WEA, and others. This was a theatre-game called 'Educational Darts'. This was created by the Great Georges Centre, a kinetic arts body with Bill Harpe its main inspirer, which is situated in the Educational Priority Area, and which is committed socially and artistically to the people among whom it exists. Drawing on their ripe experience of theatre-games, the Great Georges Centre created an elaborate metaphor of the imbalance of educational opportunity. On entry, the random flight of a dart indicated the chance birth of each participant and his inclusion in one of four classified darts' leagues. In these, to the accompaniment of Radio Topscore, with its pop music, its exhortations and its announcement of results, participants played out a heavily-weighted set of varied darts matches. Social intercourse among leagues was frowned upon and other badges of distinction – glasses of sherry for League A, inferior materials for house building for League D – were gradually introduced. It was an open-ended situation wherein varying conditions, ranging from incipient rebellion to total resignation, prevailed, and the game was closed with a discussion on the meanings, symbols and lessons of the game.

It was a most unusual device for drawing attention to the problem of educational and social inequality. As might be expected, 'Educational Darts' operated – as was its intent – at a number of levels. As expected, people reacted differently. Some found it telling and enlightening; others found it boring and even irritating. A piece of research done on the Show, however, pointed out the multifarious ramifications of the theatrical happening such as this. It had emphatic effects not only on members of the audience, but on members of the twenty-strong cast who were welded so succinctly into a well-knit team. The educative results were, therefore, many and varied.

A major drawback of 'Educational Darts' was an economic one. It was expensive. It ran for four Shows, with about 160 participants, including professional workers as well as residents, in all. Even with loaned video-tape equipment, it cost some £250 and this was getting too near to £2 a head for the comfort of the social intervention entrepreneur. It was static. Its equipment and scene-setting was colourful, clever and trendy, but once fixed it was difficult to move it. There are many possibilities in this very fascinating vehicle of the theatre-game, but, for general use, a cheaper, mobile version – one that can nip quickly into the pub and club or halt outside the school gate as parents assemble at home time, or perhaps begin with its stimulus a series of discussions – is an urgent requirement.

Still, from holiday games and door-knocking to radio and theatre, the adult education component of the project enjoyed an interesting life. It amply justified our claim that community education is a lifelong process and it demonstrated some clear pointers as to how the process should be charged.

Teacher-education

Again, the period prior to September 1969 was one of trial and error. The colleges had the valid excuse that we had caught them in the middle of the academic year, with timetables and courses beyond reform. The new academic year separated the men from the boys; it demonstrated those whose commitment was high and those whose commitment – through differing sets of priorities or circumstances – was low. We were especially keen to press the need for EPA option courses. It followed with an inherent logic that, if there were to be EPA areas and within them EPA schools at some variance with other schools in whatever way, then EPA schoolteachers might require a bias or option within their certificate course and better to equip them. With statutory salary increments for EPA teachers and the possibility of other differences in EPA schools, there was a strong theoretical argument. There seemed no reason why, as well as the conventional divisions by chronology or subject found in colleges of education, there should not be sociological divisions, catering for the requirements of especial communal typologies. With the trend towards the Community School this was becoming fast a general, not just an EPA point. More empirically, teachers in the area were wont to argue that their colleges had not prepared them adequately for the 'cultural shock' of EPA teaching. This applied to the difficulties, for instance, of upper junior non-readers as well as the problems of social background. The teacher, of course, rarely speaks flatteringly of his alma mater, and here there was some overlap into the general criticisms made of teacher-education. Certainly, however, as with everything else in the system, what weaknesses existed in teacher-training were accentuated in EPA schools. If colleges spoke of children as though they were a new species about to land from a faraway planet, then this abstract formula, this divorcement of theory and practice, was bound to have its worst effects where the problems of practice were uppermost.

In turn, if student groups were working a day or so a week in the project schools, they obviously required time for refreshment and preparation back in the colleges. They needed pre-match talks and post-match conferences. Ideally, this meant students grouped and timetabled together for much of the time. Our suggestion was of an EPA option group which enabled this combine of theory and practice to occur, and with the principles and method of education geared towards the actual project work of the students. Colleges reacted variously, as was to be expected. Edge Hill College, Ormskirk, gave a sturdy and exciting lead in the first year, with a team of students indissolubly wedded to one of the project schools, entering into all the project activities and initiating a few others besides. The students spent up to two days a week in the school. This attachment became the equivalent of school practice for these students and, in the college, a panel of subject specialists was mounted to assist them.

Other colleges tried out attachment schemes and advanced plans for the new academic year. Notable among these was Notre Dame College, Liverpool, which became the first college in the country to organize a full-blown EPA option, by which the entire education course time of twenty-eight students was devoted during their second year to this end. The students worked three primary school departments on a project curriculum probe, and their intramural educational studies were based thereon. This enabled the general principles of educational sociology, psychology and so forth as well as the curricular and methodological studies to be drawn from the practical sessions. This completely unified scheme proved one of the biggest steps forward in that coming academic year. Other colleges preferred to leave EPA optional courses to the comparative freedom of timetabling in the third year when the students might also be expected to have a proper basis of knowledge and experience. The Ethel Wormald and C. F. Mott Colleges, both of Liverpool, decided, by and large, to adopt this method with groups of students opting for final year special courses of this kind, while a Christ's College, Liverpool, team helped with a most promising creative expression experiment in one of the schools.

The project's overall aim was to institutionalize EPA courses so that the benefits accrued from the linking of college and school might be maintained after the project terminated. It was too chancy to leave the issues to the goodwill of one or two tutors and the voluntary efforts of a few students. It was essential that EPA work, in whatever form, become an integral sector of college life. The well thought out plans of those colleges who had committed themselves thoroughly to the idea gave encouragement indeed for the future.

As it was, the Liverpool Colleges of Education made a dramatic impact on the project in its second year. Six colleges mounted fourteen student-teams on a regular basis for the project schools and also to do work in the three 'control' schools, where, by now we were attempting to reproduce some of the work already accomplished in a new situation. The upshot was that as many as two hundred students were, in a peak week, in the field as numbers of these EPA commandos, bolstering the project work in the schools, helping the schools generally in a variety of ways and culling enormous benefits from the standpoint of their personal training.

Some insight into the student groups was culled from questionnaires answered by a sample of eighty, sixty of whom were using the school attachment directly as a basis for certificate work. The majority felt that the children had gained enormously from the additional attention, but a few found the benefits accruing less to themselves, one or two, for example, finding it hard to fit in their involvement with their other college activities. Almost all, naturally enough, found in their work a useful introduction to EPA work, leading to about thirty anxious to teach in EPAs, eleven more hopeful to do so after experience elsewhere, and, equally salutary, thirteen who would not have it at any price. This, incidentally, was a broadspread of students, ranging from young nineteen year olds to much older mature students. In a survey the following year conducted with 121 students of similar range, the answers about likelihood of teaching in EPA schools included sixteen 'definitelies' (one added 'if the money's right'), eighty-four 'possibilities', nineteen 'don't knows' and only two 'definitely nots'.

The students were led by seventeen tutors who constituted the College Tutor Liaison Committee of the project. If the project was fortunate to have the aid of two hundred eagerly engaged and diligent students, it was even more lucky to watch them guided by a dozen and a half of the finest tutors in the teacher-training business. Some brought lively imaginations to the task; more brought a hardheaded appraisal of the organizational and other issues; all brought a most admirable conscientiousness. This is not intended as a literary pat on the back, deserved although that is. The luck must be underlined. Where tutors were efficient and committed, there were no problems. Where, as sadly happened on occasion, tutors were less efficient and committed, the problems were overwhelming. The point must be made that EPA teacher-education cannot afford to rely on the buffets of fortune. If the EPA option course, or its equivalent, is to become a structured part of the college pattern then steps must be taken to procure adequate tutorial coverage. There is a serious gap here in the 'large and small ants' hierarchy, pointing to a pressing need for in-service training, not only for tutors, but for advisers, inspectors, teacher-centre wardens and young teachers in the EPA situation. I was particularly pleased to be invited to help plan a one-year in-service course at Edge Hill College on the teaching of socially disadvantaged children, which could act as a storehouse and development locus for the substantial amount of theory and work being produced sporadically in this field. The commitment of the colleges was the vital factor. I soon drew up an unofficial 'First Division' table of colleges in order of their engagement, at the same time, trying to persuade myself that there were many other educational problems other than the EPA one, which the colleges had to face. As with the First Division of the Football League, a correlation quickly manifests itself, between the success of the student team and the quality of the 'managers' or, to revert to collegiate parlance, principals. By this, one simply means that, where the college principal and authorities placed the EPA issues high on its list of priorities, the efforts to clear aside the difficulties and force the pace were that much more apparent. On the whole, the difficulties were administrative ones, concerning timetabling, travel, the desires of other college departments and so on; no college ever said explicitly that it did not regard the problems as urgent. Nonetheless, by this same token, administrative barriers should have been less difficult to surmount than philosophic ones. When it mattered, a concerned college seemed able to clear the decks briskly enough. As with the First Division, there were one or two colleges fighting for the top spot, and one or two in danger of relegation.

In the third year, as part of our extension programme, we mounted some thirty college teams and the number of students involved was almost three hundred. From reports received, it cannot be doubted that, in the eyes of teachers and headteachers, the teacher-education programme was the most well-received aspect of the project. Practically every school was anxious to retain the link-up permanently and there were signs in one or two colleges that some of these findings may be utilized in the generality of teacher-education and not just for EPA purposes. In the fullness of time, therefore, the teacher-education angle could be one of the most significant parts of the project. This typifies the ramifications of action-research. What started as more or less a side-issue has leapt into meaningful prominence. It is all the more important in that this is a period when teacher-training is faced with critical review.

Secondary education

Although our remit was basically the primary school, the broad nature of our strategy also attracted us to the secondary field. In some ways the characteristics of work in this area had already been rehearsed. Paddington Comprehensive School's co-operation in the establishment of a playgroup and the creation of the 'Playmobile' illustrate the point. We were well aware that the economy is an integral part of the community and thus a focus for community education attention, and some tentative steps forward were taken with regard to our connections with industry. The Moores Company laid on an entertaining fashion show of modest budgetary demands for local parents and invited EPA children to their summer gala, while local firms planned work-experience of a properly-designed kind for Paddington's pre-schoolleavers. This was all to the good, but, as our principal link-man with Moores, Tom Ward, was first vociferously to urge, this was little more than, in his word, 'patronage', and the consequence of individuals acting in goodwill rather than as company men.

It seemed that there were four pressure points for increased attention. First, there was the basic necessity for increased resources and funds. Second, there was a need for business 'patronage' of schools, perhaps even, as with the colleges of education, to negotiate 'a continuing link' between an EPA school and a commercial company in the hope of broadening the scope and substance of the school with visits, outings, pantomimes and so forth. Third, there was the need to modulate the balance between pre-schoolleaver and employer by a harmonizing of the requirements of the economy and the format of pre-school-leavers' schooling. Here, both school and employer seemed caught in a trap of which an adherence to academic qualifications was part of the snare. To some extent, schools pursued these because it was felt industry demanded them, and industry used them as yardsticks in lieu of anything else. In priority areas, the limitations of job-expectation are an aspect of deprivation and thus, whatever chasm exists between school and economy, is widest there. Fourth (and perhaps most arduous) there was the task of appraising the parent and potential parent of the work of the schools. Simply, in exploring home and school relations, one obviously finds the 'home' at work for much of the time. Most fathers and many mothers are employed and it is at their place of employment that, somehow, home-school links had to be fostered. All in all, it was essential as one conceived of the Community School, to recall the decisive factor of the economy in that community.

Throughout the project the social interrelationship between Paddington and the John Moores Company was expanded and, at this level, it was a successful element in the project. When one recalled, however, the decisive nature of the economy within the community, one realized all too frighteningly, the vast potential in industry and commerce as yet untapped. Dangers existed. It was very far from the task of the EPA schools to produce subservient work-fodder; indeed, it was encouraging to read of employers who grumbled that creative and progressive education was producing a generation of bolshy employees – it made pleasant, if scarcely credible, reading. Nonetheless, job opportunities are too much a fact of life for the EPA schoolleaver and it would seem cruel to ignore this. Rather should one aim at closing the cleft between school and work, easing the schoolleaver from one to the other situation and yet ensuring the young person enters it critically and watchfully. On the other side, there was the issue of the social responsibility of business and of how far they were willing or able to commit themselves to social amelioration. This also included their attitude to parent links being sustained, within employment, by the schools.

It is an enormous issue. With little time, few resources and even less expertise, it was the sphere in which the project team felt most overwhelmed and nonplussed. We were rightly encouraged by the start we had made and more than happy with the response, particularly as personified by the long-sighted Tom Ward, that had opened up this whole question of the relations of education and economy. Our next reaction was to suggest, rather gingerly, that this huge question needed examining in depth, not only in EPAs, but throughout the country. For our part, we would have very much welcomed another member to the project team, one versed both in educational and economic circles, to investigate the inexhaustible possibilities of the relation between the two.

Two other elements must be mentioned. An 'environmental' course for first year pupils hit upon the idea of a guide book for Liverpool 7, the postal area where Paddington Comprehensive School is situated. This worthwhile, but arduous task, resulted in a guide book which was published by the project and widely distributed, house to house, in the area. It grew from a study of the locality and a growing awareness of, say, the troubles of someone such as an immigrant, coming fresh to the area. There was also an accentuated need in terms of it being a transitional area with demolition and changed utilization constantly altering its social fabric. The old age pensioner, faced with a destroyed wash-house, might well find a guide book reassuring. As far as we could judge, this was well-received. It was a sound instance of curriculum with social purpose, drawing on an integrated pattern of disciplines, a combine of history and geography, some field and more document research, some design, lay-out and language, as well as the obvious value of a facing-up to the environment totally and realistically. There was nothing twee about this publication. As well as pubs and betting-shops, one could now find not only where the public conveniences were, but whether they had wash basins. It was an impressive and interesting exercise.

A travelling exhibition proved to be an exciting and colourful adventure. It was decided to mount a travelling 'live' exhibition of schoolwork for the entertainment and instruction of parents and community. In support of this show, the Paddington Band, an amazingly grand bunch of young musicians, played stirring medleys, and with the vocal aid of a portion of the school choir, performed a specially-written song introducing audiences to the ensemble. The Paddington Dance Society enacted appropriate mime and dance drama, and, under the English Department's supervision, there was also amusingly improvised drama. The cavalcade was received rapturously wherever it performed. Immense credit is due to the children and teachers who organized this wonderful example of carrying the school to the community. As well as visits to industry, the school's incoming parents, old age pensioners and groups of primary teachers also enjoyed the 'Paddington Cavalcade'.

That completes a résumé of the general pattern of action. Retrospectively, two points strike me forcibly. I am, first, surprised at the number of people and agencies that became involved, and I recall, mainly with pleasure, but with occasional winces of discomfort, the juggernaut nature of the project and how, at times, being its Director was like running frantically in front of a huge, powerful and swiftly moving tram. And, second, I am amazed to tot up the nuts and bolts and assemble, in this approximate fashion, the machinery of the project. Quantitively, it appears to have been quite large, and I keep asking myself what a visiting American educationist (seemingly endowed with inexhaustible dollar wealth) kept asking me – 'how did you do so much for the money?'

It was a marvellous personal experience to direct this project, and a very happy one, despite the sniffs of disapproval from those purists locked in their academic version of 'The Forsyte Saga'. I was heartened by a tale told me by one of my favourite Infant heads. She met a former pupil, a good Liverpool-Irish Catholic woman and mother of several. 'Well, Miss,' she declared, 'you haven't changed a bit.' The headteacher thanked her. 'You never got married, did you, Miss?' said the former pupil. The head admitted that this was accurate. 'Well, Miss,' she said, 'you did right not to get married. It's much the best way . . . once you get over the disgrace.' Once over the slight disgrace of purported academic disrespectability, the way we ran the project turned out to be much the best way.

6 The Action 2
Four Case Studies

1. Pre-school provision: The Paddington Playmobile

The essential element in EPA pre-school work was and (although less so because of increased nursery accommodation) is provision. With something like only one in seven or eight of the three to five age groups in receipt of any treatment, however rudimentary, it was a work of superabrogation to speak of this or that method, of programmed learning or playways. Indeed, so urgent was the need and so lamentable the provision that one was tempted to argue that almost *any* attempt was automatically better than none and that those experts wittering on about 'standards' were entirely misguided. It seemed a little aimless to strive for perfect standards for practically nobody!

It was in an attempt to make good the deficiencies that we turned, experimentally, to mobility, feeling that, if a Playmobile could help in one situation, there was a case for a fleet of a couple of hundred such vehicles in similar situations nationwide. When the idea was mooted, the voices of gloom were dominant, raised in a clamour of prophesied obstacles, like insurance, driving, garage and service costs and so on. Luck remained our travelling companion. We obtained a retired bus from the Transport Department at moderate cost (indeed the tyres, being on hire-contract, cost more than the bus!) and, at extremely marginal costs, they agreed to garage, service, fuel and generally care for the Playmobile. After some brisk negotiations with the Licensing Authorities, during which vehicles like ambulances and snowploughs were introduced as precedents, a modest motor tax was imposed, and – as we never intended actually to move people in the bus – insurance costs were not as extensive as some people had forebodingly anticipated.

The next task was that of conversion, and the boys and girls of

Paddington Comprehensive School, supervised by the technical and art staff, undertook the job as a piece of 'community service'. I always maintained that, had the bus never left the school campus, it would have been a worthwhile project. It fulfilled the two vital necessities of community education at secondary level; that is, it contributed a benefit to the local community and, at the same time, it was of educational value to the children involved. The truth of this is borne out by the following extract from an article by the two technical teachers responsible for the adaptation. It appeared in 'Survey Four' (1970), the journal of the Schools' Council Research and Development Project in Handicraft.

Since our fourth year extended course pupils were already committed on other aspects of work it was decided to introduce fourth year non-examination boys to this problem and to call for volunteers for the project. These were readily forthcoming and a programme of work was drawn up thus:

1. Strip out all passenger seats except the rear inward facing pair which housed the batteries.
2. Remove all other fittings and fixtures not required.
3. Arrange meetings with prospective teacher/crew of the finished school to determine nature of fittings, toys, etc., required.
4. Allocate jobs to teams when final proposals were known.

As it turned out final specifications suggested the following division of tasks:

Mainly woodwork

Design and fit toy steering wheels to front of lower deck
Design, make and fit Wendy House at stair corner on upper deck
Convert infant-size desks to line side of upper deck
Provision of storage space
Re-build entrance and design and fit fold-back door
Design, make and fit gates at head and foot of stairs
Design and make slide and ladder for lower deck
Design, make and fit sand pit

Mainly metalwork

Design, make and fit pivots to toy steering wheels
Make up oil drum for slide and ladder support
Make various fittings as requested

General work

Dismantle seats and strip interior
Lay chipboard floor and skirting on two decks
Build up over wheel arches, etc.
Lay vinyl-type floor covering
Paint and decorate interior and exterior of vehicle

Facts emerging from this project

1. Projects of this nature must find their origin in a real and obvious need in the community. This leads to staff having the enthusiasm so vital in first approaches to potential volunteers. (All workers should be volunteers and not 'press gangs'.)

2. Stimulation to thought and activity is best given by allowing pupils to see for themselves the problem and the difficulties it can create. In this instance, we were fortunate in that our own home management department has a nursery school so we did not have far to go to see what activities were attractive to pre-school children.

3. When the nature of the work is known after the drawing and work schedules are able to be completed, teams will often form naturally. e.g. Some boys will feel happier at metalwork than woodwork, etc.

4. It would seem that such projects would be better timetabled, rather than being dependent upon such time as staff and pupils can give. This does create great difficulties, both in staffing and in forming a special set of volunteers. It is, nevertheless, our intention to try to accomplish this on our next venture: the equipping of an adventure playground on a site close by. We may then be able to plan ahead with more certainty and the whole project should move ahead more rapidly.

5. The extent to which 'whole involvement' can be true depends largely upon the time factor. Should time be limited, then certain facts may have to be presented to teams, thus limiting the true potential of pupil investigation. Sometimes, when undertaking community service projects, it may be necessary to guide pupils at a fairly rapid rate to possible design solutions. This is by no means ideal, as the pupils should start by coping with the problem themselves and subsequently the solving, costing and purchasing of materials.

6. One can see the possibility of this kind of community service project forming the basis for integrated courses between several departments, but great flexibility of timetable and staff movement would be one essential requirement. In our case, we were able to work with the art department who provided the attractive nursery figures which adorn the exterior of the vehicle.

In view of these latter comments it is rather unfortunate that much of the work of real value which is undertaken for the community is usually dominated by the need for urgency. The usual request is that the job should be finished 'yesterday'!

We must be sure when undertaking these projects that the technical department is not being used only for the facilities it may offer, but that these projects are based on a sound educational, aesthetic and moral basis. In this way, the department, the children in it and the community will gain and be the richer for it.

The evaluation of gain on the part of those pupils working on the project is far more difficult. So many older boys seem loath to show their deepest feelings. However, we can say with certainty that most of the boys were extremely keen and proud of their individual contribution. Volunteers for after-school sessions were readily forthcoming.

This kind of work gives boys far more scope in experience of work, not readily available in the workshop. They can see how the facilities of the workshops can be adapted to circumstances arising from problems in their own allotted task. Even a potential vandal's strange urges may find some outlet in removing the seats from a public-service vehicle. (The difference between 'dismantling' and 'wrecking' was pointed out at the onset of Phase I!)

Surprisingly, in some instances, boys were able to suggest some basically sound and original solutions to design-problems, e.g. the difficulty in siting the slide was overcome by two boys obtaining and modifying a large oil drum. This was subsequently also used to support the small climbing ladder. Most boys saw fairly promptly that the prospective clients would be very small people and that this had great importance in the design of all furniture and toys. Boys found themselves thinking outside their own part of the job since there was a great interdependence across the different tasks. This kind of activity may bring an understanding of other people's work problems. This is an aspect which usually finds no real importance in the individual class job.

Another piece of good fortune was the recruitment of John Lawless, a retired heavy-vehicle driver and son of one of the Paddington technical staff, as driver, and he thereafter developed into an effective 'grandfather-figure' for all the groups using the bus. The art department completed the gay decor, inside and out; we obtained a clutch of busmans' hats for the children to wear (they went well with the four dummy steering wheels inside the bus) and Councillor Mrs Simey, a member of the Liverpool Education Committee and Vice-Chairman of our Local Steering Committee, launched the Playmobile with a suitably diluted bottle of welfare orange juice.

The Playmobile has engineered its lumbering way through a number of vicissitudes since it entered into its worthwhile retirement, but it is worth reporting on its initial three standpoints.

Our first contact led us to a lady who was eager to start a playgroup for her own children and those of her neighbours, but had been unsuccessful in finding accommodation. Parked outside her house, the Playmobile soon became known as Martha's bus and a complete group of children soon gathered, meeting three afternoons each week. Mothers helped in turn and one had appropriate qualifications. We were soon aware that they would cope on their own and we helped to find a hall into which they could move. The mothers collected a small sum of money at each meeting towards equipment for their permanent headquarters.

The next 'patch' was different. We chose an area of redevelopment some five years old. We sought out the lady on the fourth floor of the eleven-storey block who was Secretary to the Residents' Association. She confirmed that pre-school provision was insufficient and she very much welcomed the Playmobile as a support until other premises became available. Our Playgroup Adviser, Eleanor Connor, spoke to a little child playing among the rubbish and broken glass and asked him to take us to his home. A brief conversation with his mother and our first child was 'registered'. His mother also told us of neighbours and within thirty minutes Eleanor Connor had fifteen names and had promised to arrive a couple of days afterwards at 10 a.m. Eleven children arrived, eighteen the next day. We realized we could have filled the bus three or four times over and we had, in effect, started a playgroup without trying.

For the third stand we selected a space amongst a pre-war flat development, solid and dreary. We knew that there were two playgroups nearby and we aimed to use the bus as a means of recruitment for these. Again, Eleanor Connor recruited easily.

Girls from Paddington School helped to supervise these bus groups and seemed to enjoy it immensely. These third year girls suggested an 'end of Summer Term' party for one group, and this proved a very gay affair.

Apart from practical difficulties like drivers falling ill, lack of staffing and so on, one of the more pleasant problems was the possessiveness of groups. Our aim was to fill that nasty hiatus between the initial enthusiastic burst to start a playgroup, and its actual establishment – a gap usually characterized by disillusion about premises, funds and support. The Playmobile could not only give support to such nascent groups, it could also act as a barker for custom, for the sight of that huge, coloured bus in the back streets of Liverpool brought plenty of mothers and children running. But both children and mothers became overattached to the bus, and were loath to see it disappear. Still, this is a good fault, and, without reservation, the comments were all favourable. The Playmobile undoubtedly made an impact wherever it toured.

It was also our finest publicity-monger. It has appeared ten times or more on television, it has a thick newscuttings file and it is rumoured that it won't talk to the other buses now, as it proceeds on its stately way with a smug expression on its bonnet. Recently refurbished and redecorated by another secondary school in the area, it has now entered its fourth year of nursery service, and its value in stimulating interest generally in the EPA project and, specifically, in pre-school provision is inestimable.

It has been flattered by imitation. The Ealing Playmobile was its first colleague, followed quickly by one in Sheffield. Rochdale plans to develop one a year and Coventry has a Playmobile in its Hillfields area. Ulster has no less than five, three in Belfast and two in Londonderry. The Playmobile helped to present 'nursery education for all' petitions to Westminster. Obviously, these later models improve on our first pioneer design, but the principle holds good. The business of taking children to and from playgroups can, for the mother of a large family, be an exhausting affair, perhaps involving four journeys from the top of a block of flats and back, all for a couple of hours in a church hall. One has to be very convinced of pre-school education to sustain that, and there are, of course, many other reasons why there are vacancies in some playgroups and insufficient places elsewhere.

The Playmobile has shown that its flexibility can help meet the variegated and swiftly-changing pattern of pre-school needs. It is the principle of Mahomet and the Mountain. One takes the playgroup to the people at the point where it is most needed. An optimum of fifteen and a maximum of twenty can, in a well-designed Playmobile, enjoy pre-school education and act as an agency for mother-education at the same time. So far, no Authorities, be they police, education or social services, have found fault. Safety precautions are sound, and the only slight accident so far was to an adult sightseer; we park strategically by a friendly open door with welcoming lavatory; and, to avoid legal quibbles, we never offer quite two hours' provision. The Playmobile cost less than £500 to purchase and put on the road. It is an enterprise cheap and exciting enough for many organizations (colleges of education, for instance) to mount and operate. It is obviously as viable in rural as in urban districts, and its whole ambiance is rich in value and vitality for everyone concerned.

2. Curriculum development: 'The Day of the Disaster'

It should now be apparent that our regard for curriculum development was rather keener than those interested in community education mainly from the viewpoint of using the school for community activities. Even given a wider appraisal of the community-oriented syllabus, the emphasis has been on the secondary school, and our efforts in the primary schools meant that teachers saw in this approach a somewhat novel trait. Our call for a familiarization with the environment for clearer understanding as the base for sharper action, was a controversial one. It was argued, first, that junior children were not 'ready' for such sophisticated operations; second, that we should not remind them of the sordid side of their lives, or forever, as it were, rub their noses in such nastiness; and, third, that the 'basic' subjects should take preference. Our answer was that, tragically, children were all too ready, because of the severity of their circumstances, to tackle social education and that it was being kind to be cruel to take avoiding action. The idea of offering children an escapist hour or so is, of course, well-intentioned, but it adds up to little enough in hard, utilitarian terms for the future benefit of the pupils. As for the 'basics', it would be my own contention that these are most fruitfully taught in their realistic exercise – that is, reading, writing and arithmetic are best developed by a relevant engagement with the social experience of the child. Moreover, social education is so important it should be a 'basic' and possibly *the* 'base'.

We did have two advantages over those attempting similar work in the secondary schools. The primary timetable is infinitely more flexible than that of the secondary school, with its departmental strangulations, and, wryly, the nine year old getting steamed up about, say, housing or the police, is not as threatening a prospect to the teacher as the sixteen year old similarly angered. Thus, the primary schools found it relatively easy to fall in with our schemes, especially as it became increasingly obvious, progressive primary methods were ideally suited to them.

'The Day of the Disaster' is a good illustration of most of these points. We had become aware that creative methodology was most apt for environmental work and that primary teachers enjoyed and were accustomed to that approach. Our somewhat worthy and earnest 'social studies' techniques were, well, worthy and earnest. They would suffice, but as we watched and heard the children talk, model, play, paint, make music and write creatively about their locale (and, significantly, as we noted how much more interested parents were in that sort of activity), we realized that creativity was a valid key to articulate social response.

The two springs of our thinking and action in curriculum development – the need for social purpose and the value of creative expression – combined most vividly in 'the Day of the Disaster'. This was a piece of theatrework undertaken by Paul Harman, Educational Director to the Liverpool Everyman Theatre and three other actors, in over twenty junior schools, and it proved as exciting and as far-reaching as any of our curricular work.

The lead-in discussions were salutary. On the one side, the theatre group were anxious to engage in activity of an ongoing nature, avoiding the once-off character of much of their work. It was their lot often to receive all audiences in the theatre or visit one in the school, there to perform once and bid farewell to the clientele. The idea of theatrework which fitted into the implementation of a more general concept in a number of schools had an evident appeal. On the other side, we were as anxious to observe how, under such professional supervision and uniformly over most of the participant schools, children would react to social theatre.

Initially, the type of drama was not particularly material to the actors, as long as it was appropriate to the general tenor of theatre for children, whereas we wanted a specialized sociological-orientation. Our opening gambit – a deep-end jump into the immediate issues of housing – was met by a shallower paddle into historical – in this case, the Irish migrant wave of mid-nineteenth century – analogy. Their view was that this was less harsh and disturbing for the young child; our view was that an antiquated metaphor was rarely recognized by the young child. A test-case (a Roman-British conflict produced for Midland children in the hope of pointing-up immigration problems) was discussed, and it was agreed that the young audience, although enthralled by the spears and helmets, had given no thought to the Pakistani arrivals in their town.

Points were conceded on either side, and it was agreed to produce a stylized offering, with something of an Irish flavour and with a direct instance of a recent Liverpolitan disaster. The brief foreword to the score and more schools who took part might speak for itself:

The idea of the story is based loosely on the invasion of Liverpool by Irish immigrants after the potato famines of the mid-nineteenth century, and explores the sort of conditions which lead to overcrowding and friction. The disaster is the collapse of a house overcrowded with poor families – an event which actually occurred in Fern Grove, Liverpool, 8, in 1969. The events in the programme will be acted out in an idealized place and time with three locations, *Country, Ship* and *City.*

The programme uses two top junior classes, each of which is prepared for the role of *Country* or *City* people. We actors then bring the two classes together and lead them through a number of conflict situations. We tell the children that we are acting out the events leading up to 'The Day of the Disaster', so that judges – class teachers and any adult visitors – can help us to decide who was to blame. We have roles which allow us to stimulate the children to dramatic activity, within the framework of a story, while retaining control. Preparation is not necessary, beyond telling the children that we shall be coming to make a play with both children and teachers. Teachers might like to have ready questions about housing conditions.

The visit

1. There are THREE work periods of 35 mins. each, preceded by arrival and unloading period.
2. We shall arrive about 09.20, i.e. during FIRST LESSON, lunch break if we are visiting you in the afternoon.
3. SECOND LESSON is for the warm-up and rehearsal of the children's 'roles' in the play. Classes are separate.
4. Normal break to fit your routine.
5. THIRD LESSON – both groups in the hall for the play.
6. FOURTH LESSON, or till the end of the day, is the Tribunal or discussion section.
7. We should like the class teachers to be 'Judges' here, leading the discussion and encouraging a flow of contributions from all the children.

Follow-up work might include a project to find out who owns the house or flat each child lives in, what it costs and how the houses vary in size and state of repair. Art work might be interior and exterior Colour schemes.

The loosening session was very useful. Children came to know the two actors leading their group and warmed evidently to the task in hand as they prepared for the major improvisation. Paul Harman represented the 'system' – he was landlord of the 'country' land and cottages, owner of the 'ship' and property-holder of the 'town' houses, with all these facilities simply eked out with ropes, gym mats and so on. Songs were intermingled, and tape-recorded effects were an inspired addition. Crops failed and the country-folk had to migrate, unable to pay their rent to Paul Harman; the town-dwellers were unemployed and they, too, were unable to pay rents; they were thus employed to sail the ship which transferred the rural inhabitants to the urban setting (complete with a storm played out by the children with considerable bravura and mal de mer); there accommodation was so limited that families had to double up; this led to the inevitable collapse of one of the houses; and, finally, Paul Harman was hailed before a tribunal of teachers and other adults to be assessed as to 'his' culpability for the disaster.

It was an overall success from all points of view, including the huge enjoyment of the children, their lack of self-consciousness, their enthusiastic and gifted responses, the approval of the teachers and the splendid follow-up work that ensued. What came over most strongly was the children's ability to cope with these concepts. The elan and aplomb with which nine-year-old children handled rents, unemployment and so forth was quite startling. Paul Harman found himself 'moved on' and eased out by Juniors unwilling or unable to pay the rent; one group suggested breaking up his ship and selling it for scrap in order to make good the economic leeway – a solution which practically stopped the play – children, with only a rubber mat to symbolize their house, were able to smell, touch, react to and describe hideous living conditions.

I was reminded of one staffroom where I was chastised for our 'Streets Ahead' game, on the grounds that children could not grapple with items like supermarkets and public houses. I asked what hymn had been used that morning. It was 'Immortal, Invisible, God Only Wise, In Light Inaccessible Hid From Our Eyes'. Practically every word of that hymn is incomprehensible to a child. Two wrongs don't, of course, make a right, but 'The Day of the Disaster' indicated that one of these wasn't a wrong. Both from our own observation from reports received and from the conference of teachers we held at the end of the run, the same message was forthcoming. Whatever the distressing reasons for the children's social experience being so acute, it was definitely sharper than that of many middle-class children who, despite possibly higher norms in literacy and numeracy, are often sheltered and inhibited in knowledge of the socio-economic world.

'Look at that girl', said one teacher to me, pointing out a half-caste ten year old, responding beautifully and articulately in this situation and giving a bright lead to her compatriots. 'Her father's in and out of Walton Gaol and she has a reading age of five point something.' In socialized drama she was, if you like, 'top'; and this was repeated over and over. The Everyman Theatre education group realized the potential that was there; they did not make the mistake of attempting to realize the potential that was elsewhere, in suburbs culturally far-removed.

The actors were, above all, excellent teachers, drawing responses unequivocally and fluently from children, never embarrassing and never over-controlling. Had we been aware enough of the influence of such a stimulus, we might have prepared follow-up material. We made good this omission the following year during the pilot run of 'Auto-Suggestions', a kit for the study of the motor car as an urban problem. In this, two methods were pooled. We had produced kits before, but a project or centre of interest needs an explosive send-off, and a dramatic improvisation ensures a wonderful impetus. Similarly, a volatile theatrical 'happening' demands first-class follow-up, so, with our now published 'Auto-Suggestions' kit, with its five sections of activities, each including three sub-sections, we attempted just that. Paul Harman and his colleague, Bob Thompson, created a simulation, a car game played on a huge sheet of black polythene, marked out with one-wap streets, garages and shops. Children rode in Tripak motor cars on given errands, and, in trying out routes, dramatic confrontations and other traffic incidents occurred, dutifully marked by child stewards. The actors were also on hand to assist in schools anxious to develop the theatrical possibilities of 'Auto-Suggestions'. Indeed, Paul Harman's work has proved so impressive that, in our new post-project's dispensation at 'Priority', I have been most anxious to employ him fulltime, partly in a training capacity for teachers.

This anxiety must serve as an outward sign of my faith in the creative media as a vehicle for social or community education. It has the added advantages of being attractive to parents and highly diverting for pupils. I am convinced that it should much more fundamentally be utilized as a prime mover of the primary and secondary curricula. By this, I mean an integrated assault – music, art, dance, creative writing, as well as theatre – of the creative energies on probing social problems, first to understand and then to resolve them.

This reveals a movement certainly in my own and, I think,

generally in the tone of the Liverpool Project. At the beginning of the Project we canvassed the view that the study of the social environment was crucial and, over a number of schools we looked through the lenses of traditional subjects at that issue. I think we expected that the social studies, the normal history/geography kind of methods, would be most practical. For one thing, we had underestimated the amount of creative work which the modern primary teacher introduces into social studies, and, in turn, we were amazed by the manner in which children, faced with creative challenges about firsthand experience, were able to 'articulate'. Nor was it all non-linguistic; the Project teemed with examples of incisive and imaginative writing, evoked by the stimulus of immediacy. Over the three years, conviction grew that, more and more, it was this kind of talent that needed to be liberated and this kind of tool that needed to be primed.

We set our stall for social environment as the basic commodity on the educational market; by the end of the Project, creativity was accepted as the chief selling technique. We had an aim; we proposed a content; now we suggested a particular method as the chief instrument. It was when creative expression was most nearly allied to social purpose that our curricular ventures most approximated to the ideal.

I was amused, during a lecture near Darlington, to hear a student's shocked comment after seeing 'The Day of the Disaster' on film. 'I agree,' she said, 'with the Free Schools and so on; they're trying to help the child and the community that's Socialism. But I don't like what those actors are doing; that's Communism.' It was a clumsy comment, but it caused one to wonder whether the girl had blundered onto a great truth. Our hope for urban regeneration is assuredly long term, possibly more so than the occasionally restricted horizons of the voluntaryist educators. Yet it is no sort of 'Communism' in any pure sense. Paul Harman was teaching social criticism, without which communities can hardly hope to prosper and meet difficulties. If a young teacher-student could react violently, then the major problem of persuading teachers and society that the teaching task should be that of social explorer is a daunting one. And if a young teacher-student could feel menaced by nine year olds discussing immigration and overcrowding, how would she feel about the sixteen year old debating a similar issue?

I regard this somersault in the teacher's role, from, by and large, supporting the status quo to, more than hitherto, helping the child to criticize it, as the chief barrier between the idea of community education and its realization. There are considerable pressures, social and professional, on teachers to attempt a preservation of conventions and attitudes, beatified, in theory, by tradition. However outworn these might be and however hallowed in the breach rather than in the observance by the majority of their countrymen, teachers are expected to act as moral and social samplers for their pupils. Indeed, recent troubles and problems have led to pleas, inside and out of schools, for increased discipline and application of standards. So it is with no show of sunny optimism that one proposes that teachers should lead their pupils in a social critique of their surroundings and the forces determining it. It is a task at variance often with the teachers' training, sometimes with their predilections and frequently with the public mood. What it amounts to is a change in 'standards' and the recognition that the noblest teaching virtue should be an ability to look, with a tolerant balance of compassion and dispassion, at the children's society and to offer children those social competences which might enable them to come to *their own* terms with it.

Each time this approach is thwarted, such slogans as 'educating for democracy', or 'teaching them to stand on their own feet', or 'teaching them to have a mind of their own' grow more hollow. Social education – the critical curricular aspect of community education – is the making real of most of those educational aphorisms to which we are wont to pay lip-service. It is not easy, and it can be explosive, especially for those social educators who are convinced that the only answer is to reform the public system and who eschew the tempting siren calls of the deschooler. Yet when one recalls the excellent social education work at primary level of people like Frank Harris in Liverpool, or, at secondary level, of John Rennie in Nottingham and Coventry, one is convinced that we are discusing eminently practical possibilities.

It is sometimes suggested that such 'social engineering' is an unwarranted interference. What a backfiring charge! Although schools, as we are well aware, are low agents of social change, they do attempt 'social engineering' willy-nilly. It may be negative and even unwitting, but schools and teachers are always trying to impose some kind of a social mould on their pupils. What happens is that many teachers take their 'mould' so much for granted that they fail to realize it is based on their own value-judgement – for instance, the way children should grow up to behave as adult both as citizens and workers.

Certainly, I hope my colleagues and I don't make the same mistake. Ultimately it *is* a value-judgement, this belief that children should be freed, through an exercise of social skills and an improved grasp of their social world, to invent something of their own futures. Our belief is succoured by the views that, in so changing the education system, it would align it more adequately with a society where democratic notions of independent assessment, choice and decision-making are applauded; and it might prove socially necessary so to implement in practice the widely-held doctrine of social justice and equal opportunity in order to stave off urban calamity.

3. Home and school relations: The T. J. Hughes exhibition

All our home-school programmes had two main factors: an attempt to place the parent in a learner-situation so that he or she might better understand the educative process and an attempt to find natural social loci for that situation. The important premiss was the saleability of education and the fact that, granted the use of correct techniques, working-class parents could be interested and engaged in education. The national parent survey conducted by the Project was an early and precise indicator of this truth, so often ignored by many inside and outside education. I am indebted to Keith Pulham for the following clearcut account of the Liverpool sector of what was a most complex piece of social research:

200 children were selected from a one-in-twelve sample of registers in the Project schools. Five areas in all were surveyed nationally, and in total, 969 questionnaires were valid. 191 of these came from Liver-

pool. 180 of the interviews were with the child's natural mother, and the sample was drawn over the full infant and junior range. Thus, there were roughly 30 interviews in each year group from 5 to 11. 53% were boys and 47% girls. 38% of the families had three children or less, and only 5% of the sample were only-children. 62% of the families had four children or more, indicating a high average family size. Further background information revealed that 74 mothers were working, most of them in unskilled and semi-skilled occupations. 13% of fathers were unemployed, and only 31% in skilled manual jobs. The overwhelming number left school between the ages of 14 and 15, and only 5% stayed on beyond 16. 32% of the families interviewed had lived in the area for a period of between 5 and 10 years, and 30% over 10 years. 50% had grown up in the area and a similar percentage had relatives nearby. 25% of the parents had been to the same school as their children, and 72% of the children sampled were at the school which had educated or was educating their brothers and sisters.

Rather surprisingly, 46% of the mothers claimed to help their children in a formal sense to prepare for school; 56% said they had a dictionary in the home, although only 27% used it regularly. 62% had bought 'proper' books for their children in the last twelve months, although only 5% were members of public libraries and 60% didn't read books. Only 2% took a 'quality' daily newspaper, and as many as 31% of homes took no daily newspaper and 70% no Sunday newspaper. 43% of parents had hobbies which their children could follow, which were mainly of a practical kind, but there was virtually no affiliation to local clubs, societies and church activities. Whereas such cultural equipment and affiliations, which are typically part of the middle-class home environment are lacking in EPA districts, the survey did reveal a real interest of parents in their children's education. One has to ask, in this connection, the extent to which this interest is fostered by the school. A teacher-attitudes survey had revealed the almost 100% agreement by teachers that it was helpful and enlightening to talk with parents, and most disagreed with the statement that parents tried to meddle too much in their child's education.

We attempted to measure the extent of home/school dialogue. In the first place, 57% of parents correctly identified their child's class teacher and 86% the headteacher. 64% of mothers had talked with the headteacher when their child first went to school, but on the other hand, only 22% of fathers had been able to go to the school. 54% of mothers had been to at least one Open Day or similar 'formal' school event, and 77% to medical examinations. 90% agreed that it was easy to see teachers if desired, and 26% agreed that they might be interfering if they went to school uninvited. 80% agreed, in part, that teachers seemed very pleased to see them; a similar proportion agreeing that teachers were interested in what they had to say about their child's education. An overwhelming 91% were quite happy with the present arrangements to see the headteacher. As a further measure of satisfaction, 75% felt that their children were obtaining an education as good as most children in the country, and 65% felt that it was better than their own. What changes would parents like to see in the schools? 25% were seemingly content with the present situation; 23% wanted smaller classes and 16% more information from the schools. Only 8% opted for more discipline, and 6% mentioned specific curriculum changes. There was, on the other hand, an almost 100% recognition of the importance of schooling for their children and, on the whole, most parents would rather see their children doing well academically than performing well in games or household skills.

There were one or two questions aimed at assessing the areas in which either they or the school should take responsibility in the education of their children. In matters of teaching children the difference between right and wrong, keeping out of mischief, public behaviour and good manners, parents were more in favour of home responsibility. But the school was expected to take joint responsibility for correcting speech, socialization and the teaching of useful things. It was the school's sole responsibility to educate children in order to obtain good jobs. In connection with the latter point, 45% of parents wanted a 'decent' or skilled job for their child, but on the other hand, 31% were quite happy that he or she should leave school before the age of sixteen. In response to questions designed to estimate parental knowledge of the school, some of the results were quite revealing. 45% of parents admitted to problems and difficulties in their children's schooling, the most significant of which were relationships with other children and general anxiety. Only 4% mentioned the arduous nature of the work, although the general level of performance in EPA schools would indicate real difficulties in this direction.

70% of parents said that they were quite ignorant of the methods used at school, but were, nevertheless, satisfied with the progress being made by their children. An overwhelming 96% were willing to attend meetings at the school on method, and, ideally, these would be arranged on week nights between 7 and 8 p.m. The degree of parental interest can be further measured by the extent to which parents would be willing to help at school. 70% were prepared to assist in one way or another, principally with play-ground supervision, dinner duties, collecting for charity and showing people round on Open Days. Very few were interested in assisting as auxiliaries in the classroom.

This survey has confirmed the real interest of parents in their children's education, and the challenge which this presents the schools in both transmitting information and harnessing parent support. Skill and knowledge are by no means exclusive to middle-class areas, and our EPA parents have much to offer.

This survey, as Keith Pulham suggests, emphasized what, over the Project, observation bore out. A valuable potential force and ally exists among parents, and most of our home and school work was based on and fed this notable fact. At the halfway mark of the Project, we promoted our largest single event, an exhibition at the department store, T. J. Hughes. Before and since, we tried several differing places for expositions of schoolwork, factory canteens and bingo halls among them. But our first venture was with shops and that from Salisbury school along the row of shops that served the school's mainly highrise catchment area.

I remember the young teacher telling me how foolish she felt approaching the shopkeepers. She waited until the shops were empty of customers before making her bid. The shopkeepers were sceptical. 'We've been putting up stuff here for twenty years and no one takes a blind bit of notice,' said one. But, in three shops, they let her try, with a meat project in the butchers and a fish project in the fishmongers, this latter set off with a 'junk' sculptured fish (manufactured from a motor bike petrol tank with bicycle bell eyes) on the slab next to the haddock. It was an immediate roaring success, with people asking for copies of photographs and going into shops to view without purchasing; still, the shopowners didn't mind as long as the shop kept busy.

It snowballed quickly, with shopkeepers angrily marching up to the school and asking why they hadn't been included. 'Is it,' asked one, 'because we're Catholics?' Soon, with the help of a student team, there was a weekly exchange of exhibits in twelve shops, two pubs and a doctor's surgery. Sophistications developed. Sports material made for a conversational gambit in the public houses; impact material was necessary in shops, where customers were in and out quickly, whereas the doctor's surgery, with a 1940 edition of Punch the only rival during long waits, demanded more detail. It created considerable interest and other schools followed suit – I recently heard that no less than fifty shops in the Hillfields area of Coventry carry examples of schoolwork. Shopkeepers, when interviewed, were most enthusiastic about the scheme and reported the high degree of admiration and discussion that resulted.

It was this success that led me to drop in at T. J. Hughes one June day in 1969. I'd left the office early and it was a chance call in the hope of seeing the manager. After a brief discussion, he agreed, in principle, to the idea, observing wryly, 'you might as well do it here; it's where most of your children do their shop-lifting.' So, from the 6th to the 19th March, 1970, the Liverpool EPA Project took over the exhibition area and theatre at T. J. Hughes, one of Liverpool's large department stores, in an attempt to explore the possibilities of the school reaching into the community via an important focus of community activity, and the most dramatic response to the exhibition was the often repeated answer of parents and visitors when asked whether they thought the exhibition served any useful purpose. Many said that much had changed in education since they were at school, and others that they were surprised by the amount of creativity, as against the emphasis on the three Rs which made their school life so boring. They were delighted by the quality of work shown and demonstrated. This was more than a static display of primary exhibits. We planned an 'Education Shop', a Pre-School Corner, a Secondary School Display, an Adult Education Section, and a programme of live performances.

T. J. Hughes attracts shoppers from a large catchment area. This was evident from the questionnaires completed at the exhibition. 35% of those interviewed were from outside Liverpool. The sample revealed a wide spread across the social classes, which, together with the wide catchment, reinforced the point that the venue was ideal if one wished to address a wide and broadly based audience. T. J. Hughes is now affectionately referred to as 'the Harrods of the Liverpool EPA'. A memorandum was prepared as a basis for discussion and this made the point that we were anxious to locate aspects of mutual benefit and would be prepared to modify our suggestions in order to accommodate the Store's promotional interests. A provisional budget of £200–£250 was set aside to cover such costs as the publication of leaflets and materials for the exhibition. In the late autumn, there then developed a series of invaluable briefings and Shaun Leake, an art lecturer, had now been appointed Art Director for the exhibition. With the unreservedly kind and excellent cooperation of T. J. Hughes, the exhibition grew.

An important part of the pre-planning involved the project schools, who were asked to provide normal schoolwork, rather than material specifically geared for display purposes. We wanted to demonstrate what goes on daily in the normal situation. The schools responded well, and in February, Shaun Leake went on his rounds choosing exhibits and examples. On 2 March we took over the exhibition area and began the difficult task of mounting the contributions with the aid of a team of students from the C. F. Mott College of Education. We were slightly daunted by the size of the exhibition area, but, with the help of the store's design department and store technicians, we made good progress. For any group of schools contemplating such a venture it is worth knowing that large department stores may provide design services, display materials and considerable expertise. A number of tutors involved in the Project work and one or two other experts agreed to prepare eleven leaflets, under the general theme of: 'It's changed since I was at school.' Such subjects as moving to secondary school, reading, modern maths, art and adult education were covered. These were provided free of charge at the 'Education Shop'. Volunteer helpers distributed advertising leaflets and posters in the city, and we also informed the schools that we would subsidize transport costs for parents. The LEA granted the secondment of a Liverpool teacher for the course of the exhibition, and Bill Costigan performed valuable services not only as Chief Steward, but in dealing expertly with the numerous problems which always afflict such ventures.

The official opening was quiet and uneventful. The Director of education for Liverpool, Mr C. P. R. Clarke, opened the exhibition and a box of Everton toffee made by the infants at the St Francis Xavier School was presented to him by one of those fine chefs dressed as Mother Noblett, the original Everton toffee-maker. 350 visitors came that first afternoon and we were only mildly encouraged. The first full day, a Saturday, took us completely by surprise. 2000 people attended and our volunteer team of student stewards from Edge Hill College was kept active. By closing day, we had registered 10,000 visitors, and were informed by the store that this was their most successful exhibition in terms of attendance.

Keith Pulham conducted a survey during the exhibition and, once more, I am indebted to him for much of the following interesting commentary:

We interviewed 3%, that is 340, of the attendance, and this turned out to be fairly representative. Saturdays apart, when we had 2000 in attendance, an average of 600 visitors joined us, but there was, naturally, a predominance of women. 2500 listened and watched the daily performances of the Paddington School Band and the daily 'live' demonstrations of schoolwork. Over a third of the visitors were initially shoppers who had not come particularly to view the exhibition and this was a heartening measure of 'casual' response. Only five thought the exhibition served no useful purpose and we calculated that as many as 86% of the visitors had no direct connection with the exhibition (for example, as parents of pupils in the Project schools). The answers were most illuminating: 'education should be part of everyday life and not be confined to the classroom' said a brewery worker. Indeed, many felt comfortable and relaxed in a department store and thought it a pleasing link-up of education and the public. Parents said the exhibition gave them new insights into education and they were pleased to observe their children enjoying exciting new methods. There was every evidence of a sincere interest in what schools are trying to accomplish.

The exhibition was titled 'Child in the City', and, with its emphasis on community-oriented curriculum, we were making a strong point in favour of our curricular ideas. We organized an Education Shop and, as well as the many questions answered directly, we followed up seventy questions through our mail-an-answer service. It seems there may be a role for an independent agency to which parents may reveal more of their uncertainties than to the local authority or even the school. We are sure that it would be valuable to continue with the idea of an educational advisory service, and we have all kinds of plans for so doing in the future.

An important part of 'Child in the City' was the 'live' demonstrations, which gave parents and others a chance of observing the educational process at work. As in all our parent-involvement programmes, the children showed that they are not distracted by a sympathetic audience and the teachers – even presenting infants doing physical education in that crowded store – showed that they had courage as well as manifold skill. We have had several audiences of two hundred, and one of three hundred at the height of a bustling Saturday afternoon.

We soon found, perhaps predictably, that the activities conventionally served up to parents – music, drama, dance – were the most well-attended, whereas they were somewhat uncomfortable with more academic subjects. Teachers who were conscientious enough to prepare leaflets and offer verbal explanations did especially well.

Three points are worth making. Firstly, we must, therefore, look for ways of 'selling' writing, maths, reading and so forth in a lively and visual manner. It suggests integrated activities in which, for example, music and maths assist each other whilst the two both retain their first-hand character. Secondly, this first-hand character, the child-centred nature of such work, obviously enlivened the awareness and enjoyment of parents and other visitors. It should be recalled that the world of the child is also the world of the parent, so that a community-oriented curriculum has the added bonus of helping enlist parental interest. Thirdly, if we are sincerely convinced about parental support, then one of the criteria we must use to determine our syllabus should be: to what extent will it find support or interest among parents? At the moment, that would entail, on the one hand, social studies in which parents could join directly or, on the other hand, the creative activities they so thoroughly enjoy. From there it was but a short step to our newfound faith in a combine of both.

It was with some sadness that, at the end of the exhibition, we viewed the demolition of the displays. Our substantial investment of both money and manpower had been amply repaid in terms of audience response and we had demonstrated the viability of education in the market place. In the context of a large store where one could hope to meet a most comprehensive cross-section of the public, we had succeeded in an attempt to offer a greater understanding of the education process. The school and the community had been drawn closer together.

4. Adult education: The Earle Road survey

Our adult education officer, Tom Lovett, had probably the most off-putting job of all of us. He had a study population of 170,000 and, where the other members of the team had schools and other institutions on which to base their efforts, Tom Lovett had little or nothing. His technique – the searching-out of non-formal groupings and the gradual extrapolation of problems for educational action – turned the usual practice of adult education on its head. The course came last. Gone were the advertised lectures on 'brain surgery' or 'clog-dancing', which drew few customers. We learned this the hard way. We decided on a 'Football Appreciation' course. Thousands of leaflets were distributed about soccer-mad Merseyside and the football club supporters' associations were notified. The press gave some space to the plan. The course tutor was ideally chosen. He was an ex-professional footballer, now a university physical education lecturer whose research was in the development of sport and leisure in Liverpool, and who managed the then most successful amateur team in the north-west. The course was a delight for the soccer connoisseur and films of memorable matches were booked. One person enrolled.

Faced with that sort of failure, it was obvious that Tom Lovett's freewheeling non-formal approach at school-gates and in pubs was likely to turn out more productive, and so it proved. One interesting illustration of the technique, demonstrating, as it does, the underlying potential of adult education of a community-orientation, was the Earle Road Survey.

It was decided to see what would happen if we took a block of housing and explored the adult education possibility. After all, there's nothing much more non-formal than people in their own houses. We selected a setpiece of artisan terraces, a complete unit of late-nineteenth century houses, nearing the end of its existence, divided from the rest of the district by main roads and demolition already completed, its residents awaiting decantation to anywhere on the outskirts.

There were 700 of these small terraced houses, some of them dilapidated beyond repair and the energy of the occupants to salvage them further from the ravages of environmental deprivation. Indeed, some of the cases of illness and poor conditions in these privately-rented houses that came to light were among the worst we encountered. Flooded yards forever inundating kitchens, water cut off with residents obtaining supplies from neighbours, vermin vying with blocked drains to offer the most noisome horror. Quite a few of the houses were empty or abandoned.

A team of four embarked on a house-to-house canvass with a simple questionnaire relating to post-school education. 424 were completed and these made interesting reading, underwriting, as they did, our knowledge about the early school-leaving and unspectacular academic attainment of the typical EPA inhabitant. What was immediately apparent was that not one solitary soul in an area of some thousand adults was undergoing any form of adult education. Not one was taking a vocational course, let alone a professional or correspondence course. Not one was even attending a local authority recreational course, some of which were offered in nearby centres. It was staggering.

There was a 31% interest-rate recorded by the inquiry, but quite a considerable amount of tuition was thrown in – one of the team returned on several occasions to help a man whose recent promotion at work necessitated a knowledge of decimals. Something of a consultancy service was built into the inquiry, including advice for one person who wished to study Portuguese. The survey took some time, as a result, and also because two or three visits were sometimes required to elicit replies. What surprised us was the lack of antagonism, a tribute in part to the sympathetic approach of the inquisitors. There was very little suspicion. People seemed prepared to talk at length about educational problems, and so, one way and another, the inquiry lasted two or three evenings over a period of weeks.

We then personally delivered a hundred straightforward invitations to a general meeting in a local church hall. It was like a general election day. We tried to organize a babysitting service and we knocked up like party canvassers, even using cars for the short journey. We greeted with tea and biscuits the intended students. This massive effort produced thirty-one people.

There was a general discussion, outlining our plans and inviting comments and suggestions. We had on tap students from specialist colleges of education able to offer recreational pursuits like keep-fit, cookery and dressmaking. By the end of the evening, three groups had been formed for these subjects, together with a largish group who requested hair-dressing.

Two points should be made about this domestic quartet of disciplines. In the first place, cookery and dressmaking take on quite a different aspect in an impoverished neighbourhood, where low budgets dictate stratagems of clothing and feeding families almost unheard of in the suburbs. Similarly, the weekly visit to the hairdresser, which many a middle-class housewife enjoys without regarding it as exceptional, is not so common, and in deprived conditions, well turned-out clothes and well-kept hair say much more about self-respect and character than in better appointed districts. In the second place, in the informal settings of such groups, it is possible to begin the social educational discussions which it is difficult to begin cold as the stated objective of a course. During the opening general session, young housewives spoke openly, and for the first time in a semi-public situation, about their housing conditions. A line of girls under hair-driers can be an excellent platform for a discussion on housing or some other social topic.

Four groups were established and three – the cookery one collapsed – saw through the full session and the numbers grew. They were female-dominated and an attempt to develop a masculine counterpart in a local pub was not successful – our 'pub' successes were based on lengthy wooing of the established clientele, not, as in this case, on trying to attract men into a rented room in a public house for an educational reason; it was too much like the old adult education routine. Sometimes the women argued that this was as it should be and that it was time they had an opportunity to get out of the house. The church hall and private houses were used for bases. As a real and welcome emphasis of the point about recreational leading to more socially critical activities, we later formed a most lively and active group which met in the house of one of the members and devoted itself to an energetic discussion of education and other social topics.

The major feature of this exercise was the massive injection of energy and time it cost. As a consequence of several people working with great vim over a number of weeks we were able to produce an adult education structure for forty persons. That is the measure of the effort required in a depressed community to create active interest. Several of our adult educational experiments were more significant in content and more inspiring in approach than this one, but it was precisely in this venture that we took a calculated sounding of a sample population.

It was a massive endeavour, and one perhaps not possible either of replication or long term maintenance, involving, as it did, personnel and time on a relatively big scale. There is, however, another side to the medallion. Given an estimated clientele of 850 adults in the 18–65 age range, we raised the adult education provision from zero to five per cent, and very few districts in the country can boast that percentage in all forms of post-eighteen education. It must also be recalled that several other requests for educational help and classes we were, through lack of resources, unable to meet. As it stood, it was one new adult recruit from every ten homes visited, which, if repeated on a national scale, would mean perhaps a million and a half citizens more enjoying adult education.

It demonstrated a need and it also exposed yet again the fact that the existing system does not answer it. It is a fragmented system, with several agencies – the WEA, the local education authorities' further education services, the Open University, the Extra-Mural Departments and one or two correspondence colleges, notably the National Extension College, vying for a very varied trade. One rarely finds an Open University prospectus in Liverpool 8. The image of adult education is not attractive, and it is greatly to the credit of the Workers Educational Association that they have had the courage and foresight to recognize this, and more radically to find ways of answering the problem. For a forceful onslaught, much more coordination is needed. It also needs to be substantially more positive. Adult education has tended to play a passive game, patiently awaiting the arrival of the customers. Heaven forbid that adult education should be brutally forced on the populace, but we entertain no doubts that personal needs and community needs demand urgent attention.

A more positive and a more collective approach is called for. Adult educators need to move into the bazaar and push their wares a little more boldly, rather than skulk, as if half-ashamed, in their tents. If, in a given working-class district, there could be a getting together of all the available tutors from all the appropriate agencies concerned such as the WEA or the local authority further education centres, saturation campaigns could be mounted.

They could be maintained with the intensity and panache of the Earle Road Survey. They could establish local press and radio support and enlist the assistance of voluntary bodies for, say, a two-week selling campaign. There could be exhibitions and demonstrations, a joint advertising exercise and a house-to-house canvass. One might envisage bands, processions and mock barometers to indicate registrations and so on. My childhood memories of 'Wings for Victory' and 'Salute the Soldier' weeks during the War are recalled as times when towns and cities turned themselves upside down in flamboyant attempts to collect money for the War effort. Some similar enterprise might be tried, not least to inject an air of fun and sheer pleasure into what is too frequently an over-worthy and over-earnest exercise.

There is one strict corollary. Several of such agencies would have to reappraise the substance of their offerings severely before it would either appeal to the working-class, let alone the EPA citizen or be of use to him in his day by day life, be it reinforcement of his social competence in that situation or relaxation and refreshment before the struggle is joined again. It is adult *Community* education which is our concern and much of it might emanate (as indeed is happening in various parts of the country) from the school base. But a vast and imaginative change would be required in several adult and further education bodies before the essential coordinated and outgoing programmes suggested here are implemented.

7 The Conclusion
The Urban Community School

The aim of the Liverpool Project was to arrive at some tentative guide-lines about the mechanics of the EPA Community School. To recapitulate, the policy had been an exploratory broadfront reconnaissance in the opening year; a thoroughgoing, rather more structure programme in the critical middle year, plus some interchange of successful schemes among the project schools; and a sustenance of this programme into the final year, together with a number of novel items and, perhaps most significantly, the extension of the project into the other EPA schools in Liverpool.

As a theoretical goal we had defined the Community School as one which ventured out into and welcomed in the community until a visionary time arrived when it was difficult to distinguish school from community. In the short-term, it was hoped that this would engineer so harmonious a balance between school and home that the child's education would be the more stable. In the long term, one foresaw the school as an agency, alongside other social and communal organisms, working towards community regeneration. Given this ideal, the real situation has been the circumstances in which the project schools were operating. We joined in dialogue with the schools and tried to match their pace, always provided that each step we took was in the direction of the Community School goal.

By this means, we endeavoured to relate real and ideal (to put it another way, theory and practice). A hypothetical frame of reference was established within which the action was planned and, inevitably, the theory was necessarily adjusted at the dictates of practice, just as the practice was submitted to the strictures of theory. For example, our curricular theory was based on a wholesale devotion to social environmental studies. During the 'live' demonstrations at the T. J. Hughes exhibition and elsewhere, it became apparent that drama, music, dance and art were, predictably enough, subjects that excited the most substantial parental interest. Using this as an essential criterion of curricular assessment, one was constantly inclined to recognize the need for a strong aesthetic element in the Community School syllabus.

This kind of approach requires action directors who can readily set up and monitor research and research officers who can easily indulge in action. One might argue, in retrospect, that appointments to distinctive posts – action and research – in a project like ours could be counterproductive. What is ideally required are action-research officers who see the task in unified form and are equipped accordingly with the requisite skills. Action-research must come to be seen as a third discipline in its own right and not a hybrid of the other two. This digression into the professional ethics of action-research is relevant in that, if community education is to prosper, many more projects must be floated. It must be emphasized that one of the most beneficial catalysts of educational change are project teams. The medium, as it were, is the message, and one would recommend that action-research teams should be installed to implement the vision of community schooling in Educational Priority and allied areas.

One of the first outcomes of the Project then, is the idea that projects themselves provide an educationally therapeutic service. To some degree, evidenced by our operation in dialogue with teachers and others, the projects have done what many schools and staffs would do if time, money, resources and personnel were available. A project team, acting as a vigilante or commando force, can provide the necessary slack, organizing links, bringing agencies together, financing good practice and brave attempts, cajoling and stimulating, spreading ideas and doing donkeywork. Where possible, independence is of a high priority – it has been the manoeuvrability and flexibility of the Project which has been its most useful asset. But, however financed and supervised, each LEA with a massive EPA problem, or smaller LEAs, and those with a relatively minute incidence of social disadvantage, acting in consortia, should be encouraged with central government support to establish an action team, possibly with some form of local steering committee to advise it, with such interests as LEA, HMI, university, teachers, colleges, managers, parents and commerce represented.

Its main task would be to nurse the Community School into active existence, organizing college and industrial linkages, developing teacher resources centres, arranging home and school activities, like exhibitions or newsletters, stimulating pre-school activity, advising schools on re-allocation of resources, attempting to change attitudes and so on.

But it might also have two subsidiary jobs. One could be a research function. Many of the findings of the project have been avowedly impressionistic and empirical; it would take, in any event, many years of full-run community schooling before it would be possible to test the effect on community regeneration. But the Project has opened up a quarry of research topics. Some tutors are considering a research project on the EPA mode of teacher-education, as opposed to the traditional approach. Other topics – community-based curricular developments, parental contacts, pre-school playgroup provision – now require more rigorous assessment above and beyond the more approximate measures of action-research. Ideally, the establishment of a model Community School with a very longterm research schedule is called for.

The other function would be a training one. We have talked of EPA option courses, EPA teacher centres, EPA advisors and organizers of various kinds and a whole new breed of EPA teacher. Tutors, local organizers and wardens, teachers – especially heads and deputy heads – and others called to work in specific EPA fields like the pre-school and adult ones – all these will require some form of training for, at the moment, the incidence of suitable personnel is almost entirely fortuitous. A project team might take on this training role, possibly in combine with a university or college – one recalls Edge Hill College's advanced diploma course with its 'EPA thought and Practice' option.

Such action-research teams would vary considerably in membership and methodology. Their whole rationale is that each community requires a treatment tailored to its native texture and that a national blanket-treatment would probably be stultifying. As a stalking-horse, the following team-sheet, largely based on the successes and failures of the Liverpool experience, might do service: project coordinator (preferably an 'independent' or DES appointment, otherwise at a high level in the LEA advisory service), an officer or officers responsible for research, training and college liaison, an officer or officers responsible for adult community education and school management, an officer or officers responsible for home-school relations and industrial/commercial liaison, an officer or officers responsible for curricular development and related teacher/child resources and materials, an officer responsible for finance and supplies. This team, ranging from five to eleven members, might be funded differentially (i.e. from DES, LEA, industry, other foundations, universities and the like) and this would not matter, as long as the format were well coordinated, so that the team could sustain a frontal, total and well-knit assault on the EPA. Such task-forces were emphatically proposed in the national EPA Report to the government.

We feel able now to construct a package-deal or check-list for the EPA Community School. It is founded on a collection of items from our pilot programme and it would be our contention that, if a school adopted this collection of schemes in toto, it would overnight be a radically different institution, one confidently involved in a full community education schedule. It is a package-deal which can be adopted at any level. It is our belief that it would most profitably be implemented by a pattern of task-forces as described above. Failing these, there is material here for the Department of Education and Science, if it so wished, to weave into a national 'Plowden' policy: there is the opportunity here for any LEA to take note and install such a schedule in its own locality; there are lines of thoughts and suggestions for advisors, organizers, college tutors, education officials, school managers or governors, education committee men, and even for HMIs to pop into their cross-pollination satchels; there is a formula which a headteacher could accept and modify for a particular school; while, not least, there are ideas and guide-lines for the individual teacher to adapt for a particular classroom. This sounds an arrogant boast, but it is said in trepidation and not with overweening assurance. For the aim of this Project was to recommend a national EPA policy and, if it works for the nation, it must work at all the other levels, up to the classroom situation.

The package-deal can formally be divided into four sections dealing with our chief concern, the primary school, but consideration of the three other stages of education, pre-school, secondary and post-school or adult education are essential. Although these three sections have been scantily dealt with, compared with the primary school, it should never be forgotten that community education is a cradle to grave concept, that, in the school sense, it should best be seen as a three to sixteen/eighteen continuum and that, in general, it must give the education system globally to the people, with adult education well in evidence at all stages.

The Primary School – home and school relations

It would be assumed that the school would deploy its plant for the benefit of its catchment area. It would be hoped that those concerned with school building would consider this point urgently and plan for purpose-built Community Schools. Beyond that, one might hope to see comprehensive programmes which incorporated new schools fluidly and openly into newly-developing environs. It would also be assumed that the 'open' school would play a fair part in the pre-school and post-school educational activities of the neighbourhood.

However, the main outgoing or communal commitment of the school would be in the field of improving parental and public knowledge of its activities, in order that parents and others might be better placed to support the children's education. This, substantially, is a public relations exercise, and we have indicated an approximate formula for conducting such an exercise. Set out in logical progression, it might read:

1. *The Publication.* Here, the emphasis is on the professional presentation of material into the home, and we have experimented with some success with the teacher-centred newsletter, the child-centred magazine, a mixture of these two, the one-off prospectus, the calendar, and the booklet based on a major piece of schoolwork such as a study of the locality. Expense forced the Project latterly to experiment with the common cover, 'Back

Home', (now heading towards its eighth edition), which could be used either independently or as the backing or folder for school, class or individual material of all kinds. In Liverpool this was, with its 710,000 run, a popular addition to our help to many schools and, in the main, it was used with imagination and dash. It is obviously a task for the LEA or for the recommended 'project team' to produce for a given set of schools. It could even be produced on a national basis, and one might even foresee a triple layer – a national cover, a local contribution and a school insertion.

2. *The Exposition*. It should be the duty of the Community School to sell its wares at natural focal points in its catchment area. The most obvious examples of this culled from our own experience are shops, department stores, public houses, doctors' surgeries, bingo halls, community centres, churches and factory canteens and social clubs. That in no way is an exclusive list, for supermarkets, public libraries, cinemas, races, football matches, holiday camps and many other social foci could be added. Exposition takes two forms – the straight exhibition and the 'live' demonstration – or, of course, a combine of the two. The latter has marvellous impact, especially when supported by hand-outs or other material. The former needs constant change to retain its attraction and the danger of children doing 'exhibition' work must be watched. In some ways, the 'live' demonstration is one of the freshest approaches in the school/community field and one worthy of some development.

The concept of exposition leads naturally to the 'Education Shop' idea, and the Project, in completing its operations, planned a collapsible kiosk for general use. It is felt that LEAs should look critically at such prototypes. 'Education Shops' have naturally been seen chiefly in the department store context, but there is no reason why they might not operate at other focal points, like the ones suggested above. Alternately, it would be a tremendous boost if one or other of the large chain-stores undertook to establish an 'Education Shop' in each of its branches. There is little doubt of its value but it must be seen as a long term venture. As with any other social mechanism, it takes some getting adjusted to and people who have been disappointed with a week's experiment have entertained foolish hopes of the 'Education Shop' mechanism. Since the end of the Project, we have also looked closely at the practical implications of a mobile advisory service, and the results have been encouraging.

3. *The Site Improvement Scheme.* By declaring war on their own site, teachers and children can demonstrate to the community their intention to look critically and positively at their surrounds. Playground wall-murals, litter campaigns, reclamation of bits of land for garden, roof and playground gardening, and interior decor, particularly in corridors, have been the principle illustrations of this. Ideally, they draw curricular and communal concerns together. Each piece of work grows from an intrinsic part of the syllabus, so that the adult observer, as well as noting the social value for the children and the community, is also vividly informed of what the school is attempting in a curricular sense and this, more direct, message is one worthy of further consideration. The scope for child-centred improvement schemes is broad and one should next perhaps consider a widening of this device beyond the school bounds. The Christmas decorations for a shopping precinct or a wasteland 'junk' sculpture enterprise are two examples which spring to mind.

4. *The Parent in the Process.* There is no gainsaying that, for full home/school inter-relation, the parent must eventually observe or, preferably, participate in the educational process. The Project has undeniably shown that the class is the most profitable focus for this exercise, with teacher and children inviting parents to join them regularly for half-day sessions. This began as 'coffee mornings', but widened encouragingly into the afternoon and evening. There were several permutations on the theme, but most schools plumped for the parents joining their children working in groups and the creation thereby of a valued social-cum-educational experience for everyone. The success of the evening efforts, when fathers and working mothers have an opportunity to engage themselves, might point the way to weekends as well as evenings as a viable time for schooling. Provided no increased overall burden was placed on teachers, some investigation of this possibility might be attempted, with parents and children (perhaps on some kind of roster basis) enjoying early evening and

weekend school together. This, incidentally, could be the juncture at which to mention the need for holiday programmes in the Educational Priority Areas. Given a lack of leisure facilities and a paucity of traditional educational achievement in such areas, a strong argument could be made for holiday schooling, again provided teachers were not overburdened. An evening, weekend, holiday approach should necessarily imply a close look at teacher-commitments and conditions of service, but, in terms of parental involvement, it could be essential. We have recently experimented, with some success, in the holiday school field.

With instances such as the 'festival' theme, whereby parents were invited to school to help celebrate calendar occasions which had been the recent centre of interest for the children, parental and curricular probes have been drawn nearer. But the ultimate comes only when the parent undergoes the process with the child, in what we called parent-child projects. Experience with these was limited, but hopeful. Only four were attempted; success varied; but innumerable lessons were learned. Again, a series of evenings was tried as well as a run of afternoons, and, predictably, creative and local studies seemed most suitable. It would be a significant breakthrough if schools could be encouraged to float child-parent projects of this nature, possibly attempting, initially, to ensure that every parent has at least one chance of the experience during the child's stay at school. The usual warning must be appended. It could take a generation or more of hard slogging to adapt teachers and parents in general to this final step in the partnership.

There are, we have observed, no blanket answers to home and school relations. The project team would advise all teachers to examine themselves critically before embarking on one or another scheme, for their success often depends on teachers' temperaments and personalities. Nor did the team examine all the possibilities – one thinks of home visiting (as successfully developed by our colleagues in the West Riding Project), teacher residence in the area, parents spending a day in school in twos or threes, and so forth. It perhaps should be reiterated that parent associations, parents as teacher-auxiliary or 'parent power' was not part of the thinking in this first phase. It is the fathers and mothers in the learner-role that requires urgent remedy; as such, the teacher must be seen as critical. If one teacher can be converted to good home/school practice, thirty pairs of parents and their children could benefit. If one parent is converted and becomes a proseltizer of home/school practice at the school, it could, in fact, alienate teachers.

The rapport of school and home must, of course, be the rub of any community education programme. Every EPA school must be persuaded of the import of this truth. It is, in essence, a public relations venture and, as such, resources need to be diverted for the purpose. We recommended nationally that each EPA school should be subsidized with an annual public relations grant of £150, or 50p. *per capita,* whichever be the greater. In our experience, this would enable a school to publish material pleasingly with the aid of some common 'Back Home'-type folder; to mount a small set of exhibitions and demonstrations within its locale; to embark on and sustain a site-improvement scheme; and to float a thoroughgoing parental linkage through the school. This is not to limit the school to these four techniques we found most valuable, but it does offer some reasonable base for a monetary calculation. And if the agelong dichotomy of school and home in urban centres could be broken for £150 a year, it would be indeed a cheap investment.

The Primary School – the 'community' curriculum

Having observed a number of community-oriented curricular probes, one is left with the unenviable job of constructing some artifact for general school usage. This is wellnigh impossible. The curriculum needs to be flexible, according to the nature of teacher, parents and pupils. It needs to be locality-centred. It needs to be founded on themes rather than subjects, and these could vary astonishingly from day to day and area to area. Further, curriculum development is much less spectacular than home/school development, where the response, for goodwill, is immediate and dramatic. A community syllabus – aiming at the more critical and constructive adaptation of children to environment – is self-evidently long term and not open to the conventional measurement of educational research.

At this point, therefore, only groundrules are on offer and these are four in number. First, the balance of the curricular diet should change from 'academic' to 'social', with reality-based themes (pursued over monthly, half-termly or even termly periods) forming the staple. These should become what teachers now call the 'basic' or 'bread and butter' subjects, with all else feeding in and growing out of them. Naturally, there is a firm case to be made for extensive language programmes, but, here again, it is important that these are imbued with a high sense of social purpose and that reading and writing are exercised in socially relevant material.

Second, it follows that much of the work, particularly at junior level, would have a locality basis. This should not be exclusive ('television', for example, is a non-local theme, highly relevant to the urban child) and it should always be seen as a foundation for widening outlooks in the children. Nonetheless, a careful study of their immediate environment should form the children's chief fount of inquiry and it should remain at the centre of their social familiarization. It has been argued that this, in turn, is the more likely to engage parental interest, and it is a truism of home/school practice to observe that curriculum choice is probably as meaningful as any other feature in cementing links between teacher and parent. But, as well as a capacity to involve themselves in local studies, parents have long demonstrated an appetite for music, drama, dance and art. If schools wish, then, to tempt parents, this is an extra reason for giving a substantial boost to these subjects which are not regarded in the same light as English or maths and which are even relegated to a Cinderella position. The 'social' corrollary needs to be added; namely, the use of creative pursuits to give children a chance of exploring their environment with a broad choice of media and to act as an informative entertainment for the community. This is, one is ashamed to confess, heresy for the more esoteric educational artistes, with their belief in the arts more purely as a means of self-expression. Valid as this is, in the Community School context the arts have a more socially definitive role to play.

Third, social environmental or communal studies should concentrate on skills rather than information. The teacher has traditionally noted the maturational rates of children in reading and number, but this has been less marked in humanities teaching.

Seven year old children are confronted with the Roman Empire or the African pygmy or hymns like 'Immortal, Invisible, God Only Wise; In Light Inaccessible, Hid From Our Eyes', and this is the equivalent of starting reading with copies of 'War and Peace' or maths with quadratic equations. Similarly, relatively little effort has been made to see these subjects developmentally, with due regard paid to the evolution of concepts about time, space, society and the like, along the same lines as number or word skills. Having reappraised the content in more realistic terms, it behoves teachers to use the social periods not merely as informational, but more as developmental sessions. The aim is to equip the child to look at his world more articulately and sharply, and the skills are all-important. One often hears of teachers using geography and history lessons to 'help' reading and writing, or as the basis for art and craftwork. This needs largely to be reversed, with both verbal and creative method placed at the disposal of social purpose and expertise.

Fourth, and most difficult, is the necessary change of teaching attitudes. Historically, the teacher has been cast as the defender of the status quo and, indeed, the one found culpable if social unrest, be it juvenile delinquency or drugs, threatens. EPA community education as an element in community development is about moving on, not standing still. It presumes that an Educational Priority Area should radically be reformed and that its children, as junior citizens, should be forewarned and forearmed for the struggle. This is not to expect each teacher to form a revolutionary cell in his classroom, but one might hope for an open-ended approach to social issues. The police is a neat example. It is easy enough to persuade a teacher to teach the police as a local theme, but one sees it done under the heading 'People Who Help Us', with the resultant hoarse chuckle from the children. This is not police-knocking; it is unfair to dress up the police in this avuncular, 'Mind how you go' image, rather than see them as a human institution with its own preconceptions and difficulties. Thrift is another example. From time immemorial, teachers have taught the virtue of thrift. Apart from their responsibility for all those poor old ladies who die of starvation with hundreds of pound notes stuffed in the mattress, thrift is often coterminous in working-class areas with meanness, and to be thrifty is to be castigated as a stingy bastard. Teachers, too, are frequently caught out in unconsciously hypocritical poses, as witness the teacher who after a hard day on the police and thrift, is knocked off for speeding on the way home to fill in his football pools. This is another side to the teacher who teaches Tennyson by day and watches Coronation Street by night – only it is, if anything, the teaching of Tennyson that is wrong. Obviously, the transference of the noblest teaching virtue to being a compassionate, tolerant and critical examination of all social, political and moral issues is the toughest obstacle of all in the implementation of a community-oriented curriculum. It could take years and it will require a generous and sympathetic change of heart, not only among educational authorities, but in society at large.

Granted these four ground-rules, and relating them back to the home and school recommendations, it is possible to schedule a week's junior school activity. Some argue that 'social' education is not viable until the secondary stage, where, unluckily, the fits and starts of the subject-timetable make it less possible of consummation. Our submission would be that it is worth attempting throughout the child's schooling and schools do, of course, provide social training from the pre-school and reception years. From one angle, 'social' education is the open-ended projection of this social training and the project work in Liverpool has convinced us at least that the junior child can cope with social studies admirably, provided it is pitched in tune with his conceptual levels. Moreover, there is a likelihood that the reverse is true; children seem to be late in a mastery of social skills, precisely because those skills have been inadequately exercised. Let us look at a junior school week, assuming with a sort of wry optimism, that only the pre-morning break sessions would be devoted to the rituals of religious education, reading method and maths.

One might spend the remainder of the five mornings on physical recreation and on the fairly lengthy investigation of some general social theme, such as comics, the milk bottle or football pools, with every teaching method introduced to widen and stimulate the inquiry. The afternoons might be devoted to: an intensive study of some local theme or point of interest, obviously with visits-out an intrinsic feature; a site-improvement or other 'communal' scheme; such as the running of a weekly club for old age pensioners; a parent-centred session, preferably a child-parent project; the preparation for eventual performance (on, say, the 'parent' afternoon) of some creative activity, preferentially on a social topic with inter-disciplinary media deployed; and a reserve afternoon for occasional visits, interesting visitors from the community (parents talking about their jobs is an obvious instance) and for making good time-and-motion losses over the rest of the week.*

It would be an exhausting week for a teacher, who might at this point also recall feelingly the suggestion of evening and weekend schooling! Suffice it to say that later suggestions ask for the granting of improved ancillary help to EPA schools and for the formation of College of Education task-forces for each school. A teacher embarking on such a full-run programme as the one outlined should be assured of proper technical assistance and of the recruitment of a student-team to be available on at least one full day or two half-days each week. Although we make no great claims for our curricular probes on the project, the Liverpool teachers engaged in the work have proved one thing to the satisfaction of all onlookers, as well as, more significantly, that of the children. Given the regular, well-supervised and steadfast support of a strong student team, the exploration of these social themes is practical and they are also immensely exciting and satisfying to everyone concerned. Social fare is not, as some have argued, dull fare; it enables the teacher and child to discover a mutual relevancy of purpose and immediacy of enjoyment in educational activity.

What can be done in an in-service way to procure such dispensation in the primary schools? It is apparent that a vital schedule of courses and publications and help in the schools would be required and, once again, a project team would be ideally placed to attend to that function. These teams, or, failing them, each LEA (or, for scattered EPA schools, several LEAs in concert at suitable vantage points) could establish a Teacher Resources Centre, similar to the one we have now established in the

* For the development of both these curricular and parental notions, see Eric Midwinter, *Social Environment and the Urban School*, Ward Lock Educational, 1972.

Liverpool EPA. These centres would have two allied functions. They would, by courses, seminars, exhibitions and discussions, orientate teachers to the principles and methods of community-based studies and provide opportunities for teachers to prepare their own related materials. They would produce locality-based or otherwise relevant materials for the teaching service, thus meeting the valid complaint of teachers who, while accepting the need for this kind of work, point out that educational publishers must perforce provide for a much more general and abstract market. The Liverpool Project's 'Projector' series were promoted as samplers of this function, and included kits, games and workbooks dealing with all levels from pre-school to adult. A four-volume social studies workbook has now been prepared in Liverpool. It's flexible enough to be used in any area for local investigations and also 'developmental' in that succeeding volumes are geared to the average social maturation rate of the junior child.

LEAs might be well advised to follow Liverpool's wise example and appoint an EPA teacher resources warden to co-ordinate this and other internal school action. Provided fittings, equipment and premises were available – in, for instance, a school with spare room – only one senior appointment, plus secretarial assistance, and with a modest grant for running courses and producing materials, could make it possible to organize a resources centre for as little as £10,000 each year (£4,000 salaries; £5,000 materials grant; £1,000 miscellaneous equipment, expenses, etc.). A teacher centre like this could be a first rate catalyst for curricular reappraisal and development, and it was an important EPA recommendation that proposed their widespread establishment.

The primary school and the college

On the testimony of those shrewdest of judges, the teachers and heads, the most successful component in the Project was the college-school link-up. It is not less important, nor is it entirely unrelated, that it was likewise the most inexpensive component of the Project. For sheer mutual benefit at low cost, it would seem hard to beat the 'continuing link' between school and college, with, by and large, everyone feeling some profit. During the third year of the Project we had over thirty teams in the field at one time or another and, at the peak, we mustered twenty-nine simultaneously. Nearly three hundred students were engaged in the operation. This put the lie to the Jeremiahs who had said that it was an experiment incapable of replication. In the country, there are now some two hundred teacher-training institutions (university, college, polytechnic and so on). There are less than six hundred EPA schools (although, in our view, there should be many more). Even allowing for the fact that it would be urged more schools should be designated and that many colleges are not situated within sound of EPA gunfire, the Liverpool college-school links-up do suggest that an enormous potential exists. As an underpinning of the national recommendation to this effect, the Liverpool continuation project has maintained and extended its pioneer work in this field.

It is perhaps worth recapitulating the major points. The teams must be tutor-led, regular in attendance and backed by intramural coursework. Second and third year students did equally well on these EPA Option Courses, and indications were that an optimal team number was ten or twelve and that a minimum of a day-attachment was necessary. The teams were most suitable for curriculum development and also as task-forces for special ventures – school exhibitions, school camps, school sports and the like. When the tutors and students could form a unified front with principles being drawn from practice and, conversely, being woven into practice, the situation was wellnigh perfect. An advisory panel of specialist tutors was another useful addition in some colleges. Several colleges also found great pleasure and reward in inviting classes of children into the college for the day so that a two-way relation was really instituted. Our tutors now are faced with the retrogressions and cyclic tremors of the James Report, just at a time when they seemed to be solving that problem of compounding practice and theory that the James Report assumed insoluble. However, in Liverpool this work is likely to continue and extend in no uncertain manner. Those tutors directing the EPA Option Courses had already served on the liaison committee which decided to institutionalize itself, with its own officers and policy. Its functions are: to maintain and perfect the 'continuing link' technique, employing the mechanics worked out during the Project; to act as a pressure group in college and university circles for improved resources to aid the work, e.g. to obtain firmer support from subject departments in colleges and to demand formal recognition of courses at university level; to act as a ginger group in spreading the idea of continuing links; to fulfil a role in curriculum development. This last was prompted by a late realization that dozens of students were engaged in interesting curriculum work in the school, but that little interchange took place. The tutors felt that, in conjunction with our new teachers' centre, they could become a working-party, sorting and resorting, refining and, where possible, replicating satisfactory curricular ventures for common use. The EPA students' conference, which is set fair to become a hardy annual, is one obvious point of interchange, but the tutors were determined that no chance of furthering sound curricular innovations and materials would be lost.

This had been a grassroots movement, but, in recommending the extension of this mode to colleges everywhere, one might hope for a strong lead from the Area Training Organizations up and down the country. Now that, in some variety, the technicalities of link-up with EPA schools have been pioneered, the swiftest way of transmitting the approach could be through this administrative focus around which the colleges cluster. The surest way would be by appointment of a tutor responsible for organizing the liaisons between school and college and between college and college. He would be responsible for the proper construction of EPA optional coursework in each of the colleges and its relation to the Certificate of Education. For instance, where the regular attachment has not been interrupted by the needs of a block school practice and where the theoretical studies involved have been presented for assessment as part of the certificate course, the student commitment has been heightened and his natural anxieties lessened. Similarly, each college needs a tutor or two capable of running an EPA Option Course, with theory and practice gelling tidily.

One thinks of the overseer tutor, or his equivalent, as a member of a project team. No task on the Liverpool project was more fatiguing than the marrying of colleges and schools. It also needs to be done in the context of the all round work of the enterprise; it needs, for example, to fit in with whatever curriculum and home/school action is in train. Once again, the need for a team, in which a college-school liaison person would play a crucial part, is paramount. For instance, in conjunction with a teachers' resources centre, a good tutorial committee, drawing on college support, would offer inestimable help in producing curricular materials and organizing courses.

Another urgent training need is at the higher echelon of college tutor, headteacher, adviser or teacher-warden. It is purely fortuitous that the Liverpool project happened on a bunch of dedicated and knowledgeable tutors. Good luck cannot be relied upon. With so much new thinking and action in EPA work, it is vitally important to establish training programmes for those who will be in charge of student and in-service instruction for teaching in socially deprived areas. As well as novel teaching approaches there is a whole fresh field of parental involvement with which to grapple. In the past, teachers have had little or no help with this trickiest of skills.

Certainly we should reform the training structures, with prestidigiously graded diplomas for the more high ranking educators, with, say, one term in-service courses for existing EPA teachers (perhaps using the James Report Cycle Three formula), and with EPA Option Courses for student-teachers anticipating appointments at some stage to EPA schools. One might look then, over a stated five or seven-year period, to a prescribed qualification for the EPA teacher which would enable him to earn a high annual increment. On the one side, this would give the EPA teacher a well-deserved status and bonus, on the other side, it would assure a modicum of specialized training for those attempting probably the most arduous of teaching jobs.

The Primary School and the community

In the home and school section, several facets of community relations were touched upon, leaving, nonetheless, several others quite unexamined. From any number of possibilities the project did alight briefly on two very different community features and they require some specific comment. They are school management and the economy.

First, as to managers, the Community School requires community management. It needs men and women who can act as interpreters, as bridges between the school and its locality. There is little evidence that the dominance of LEA elected members and nominees on managerial or governing bodies is able to perform this function, save in exceptional, all but accidental, cases.

Legislation should allow, as soon as possible, for a positive move towards 'community' boards of managers and pressure needs to be mounted nationally and locally to that end. A suggested panel of managers might read: headteacher, teacher representative, LEA officer, LEA elected representative or nominee as ratepayer watchdog, parent or parents, related commercial or industrial representative, where relevant, related college representative (perhaps replacing the conventional university delegate) with powers to co-opt up to three others able to meet or represent the particular interests of the individual school. A radical change in the structure of management must preface a radical change in the function of management. It is frequently difficult to find a parent who can name one manager of his child's school. Some schools are extremely fortunate in their managers and governors, but probably all would benefit from a facelift. To assist in such a facelift, obligatory courses for school managers and governors should be arranged and lists of managers' names and addresses should be widely published among parents.

Secondly, as to the economy, the happy relations the Liverpool Project negotiated with the John Moores organization were a valid reminder that the community is an economic as well as a social one. We were rightly castigated for lack of follow-up of our initial overtures. This was accurate enough and we could only plead lack of time, money and expertise to excuse us. Our frankly underdeveloped connections with industry chiefly served to demonstrate the almost frightening potential of educational/economic rapport. The four main angles appeared to be straight material support, extended social relationships on a two-way basis, parental communication after the 'home is at work' aphorism, and, in the case of secondary education, vocational adjustment and the import of narrowing the chasm between school and work. Perhaps it should be added that there was no thought here of churning out suitably moulded factory-fodder; the belief was that, as a parallel to producing the thinking consumer and citizen, the Community School should attempt to produce the thinking producer and worker, able to participate as creatively in the workplace as in the residents' association.

As a foundation for this endeavour, schools and companies could be interlocked rather after the fashion of the college link-up. In some ways, the complex economy of most urban centres makes it impossible to negotiate a genuinely direct and integral connection, analogous with the mining village with its one colliery and three or four schools. It can normally be presumed that parents attached to one school rarely duplicate the pattern at work. Nevertheless, if a group of schools were variously associated with a group of commercial concerns, a criss-cross network could manifest itself beneficially. A broad programme could be planned of financial and resources support, of worker visits to types of schools, of varied exhibition-demonstration and 'Education Shop'-type activities, of school involvement in company sports, theatrical and other social occasions, and of a variegated pattern of pre school-leaver experience. Together with a relevant business representation on school managerial governmental bodies, this could prove a tremendous advance in both the theory and practice of the Community School.

As with the college liaison schemes, such consummations do not spontaneously occur. Some kind of leg-man is required to forge such close and detailed links, and, yet again, he would ideally need to operate within a project team so that the school/work action could be dovetailed carefully into the total programme. There are openings here for local business and industrial interests to finance industrial educational officers for this purpose.

It is difficult to overexaggerate the significance of this finding. The comment here is brief because, in substance, the evidence is slight. It is truer to say that the project team merely saw a glimmer of a bright potential. One must not be naïve. Few industrialists and employers and executives are as longsighted and as aware of their social responsibilities as were our business associates. It would be a laborious slog and an often vain struggle against suspicion and short-term evaluations. One would need swiftly to draw the trades union movement into the reckoning and not be content with discussion with the management. It would be fraught with countless difficulties. Yet it cannot be gainsaid that if 'community' has meaning, it must include the economy and thus it is to the economy that community education must address itself. Given what one now sees as a remarkable, if somewhat inaccessible, potential, and granted the import one would now attach to the economic sector of the community, one might argue in retrospect that if a re-start of the Project were possible, a greater emphasis on this element would be the only basic change of strategy. Since the project ended, we have begun three schemes for unemployed school-leavers under the Government-sponsored 'Community Industry' programme, and we see this as a fruitful lead.

The implementation of this quartet of suggestions, traversing the full gamut of curriculum, home and school relationships, college attachment and community interests, would give any primary school a strong and hardy 'community' bias. The three other levels of education (pre-school, secondary and adult) must, of course, be geared in to such a development, less the EPA primary 'community' school end as a detached operation.

The community frame of reference

There are one or two further crucial points that must be discussed. As a frame of reference for the implementation of this general programme of community education, it is imperative that a return is made to the Plowden recommendation of designating Educational Priority *Areas*, rather than schools. The designation of schools has led to ridiculous anomalies, with EPA and non-EPA schools only yards apart, with departments of the same school differently designated and fringe issues like the amalgamation of two nearby, but differently salaried, staffs. Secondary schools have almost entirely been ignored, as if some divine metamorphosis overtakes the eleven-year-old EPA child – a converse, in fact, of what, according to many secondary teachers, sadly occurs. Approximately, the 570 official EPA schools represent perhaps a half of the total submitted by the LEAs in 1968, and there is a strong case for widening the scope in terms of the grey or twilight zones around the EPAs. Rural deprivation might also be given more consideration and, most important of all, there are the municipal redevelopment areas. Redevelopment – particularly its highrise manifestation – is already a feature of EPA work, and teachers have been heard to argue that their troubles only really began with redevelopment. It cannot be affirmed too strongly that the redevelopment area is often the EPA in projection, for hot water and a lavatory do not automatically solve the educational and social problems of the population in question. What one gains on the physical swings, one loses on the social roundabouts. City centres offer a rich resource frequently distant from the characteristically austere clime of the new council housing estate and its citizenry have normally been recruited sporadically and in urgent need of communal welding.

So, as the national recommendations made clear, the widening and filling out of the EPA concept is important. It is important, for example, to teachers who sometimes have an ambivalent attitude towards the EPA label, which is never far from the surface and which has dogged our efforts on occasion. Teachers enjoy a love-hate relation with the EPA idea. On the one hand, they recognize the desperate problems of the children in their care and are grateful for endeavours to resolve these. On the other hand, they recoil from the slur of the school, not the area, being so designated. However much one reminds them that the designation is based on the social background of pupils and not on the substance of the school, they still sometimes regard the label as a gratuitous insult. It is almost as though the very identification of the trouble, the very lifting of the carpet to show the dirt, somehow worsens the situation. It leads to huge contradictions when teachers talk, often within the same sentence: 'the children here are just the same children everywhere else . . . look how tired Jimmy is. His mother's a prostitute; she kicks him out of bed when she brings a man in.' Or, 'this school and its children are just as good as any other; we don't want to be picked out for differential treatment; all we want is more staff, more money and better buildings.' It is necessary to move as quickly as possible from the pre-Plowden phase of ignoring the problem, through the present phase of identifying the problem, with all its attendant discomforts, to the phase of dynamic resolution. To this end, the status of the EPA teacher (speaking now in terms of the enlarged EPA concept) must be firmly enhanced for we must swiftly breed a teaching elite, a vigilante force which will act courageously and imaginatively for the advancement of the urban Community School. One is encouraged by the wave of young teachers with a high degree both of creative and sympathetic outlook and of social commitment. If these elements could smoothly coalesce with the sensitive and mellow experience of those many teachers who for so long have, silent and unsung, held the educational and social line with such purpose and dedication in our urban districts, therein might lie the answer.

But it would be unfair as well as uneconomic to pretend that a dosage of social conscience would induce a cure. Teacher conditions must be improved, in part, because no teaching job is probably as tiring and strenuous as this, and, in part, to redress some of the imbalance of 'suburban' teachers looking down on their 'city' colleagues. As to salary, the EPA increment has been accepted with appreciation as a token of recognition, but few Heads report that it has made much difference to recruitment. In Liverpool it has been variously and contemptuously dismissed as 'dirt-money', or as travel expenses which the suburban teacher, who lives near his workplace, does not need. After all, it amounts, after tax, to a pint of bitter a day. Money is not everything, but, if it is going to enter the argument, it should mean something and society should not be coy about it. A standard increment of £250 would make the kind of decisive impact required.

Because of the fatigue of urban teaching, particularly in terms of a community bias, and because of the calls of professional status, it is essential to create much improved accommodation and services for EPA teachers. There should be a first-class staff 'sanctum', where teachers might retire for relaxation and privacy. Here, as well as excellent amenities for study and preparation, there should be topgrade catering facilities and, possibly, provision for overnight stays. Ancillary staff for welfare, clerical and technical assistance should more abundantly be provided. In composite terms, there should be an ancillary worker to every three or four teachers. In brief, the poor conditions that are too often the lot of the children, also adversely affect the teacher, who finds his or her staffroom cramped, ill-equipped, used as a spare classroom and so on. If we are to expect teachers not only to be attracted to EPAs but to operate productively when there, a radical improvement in their working conditions is a proper pre-requisite.

There is a sharp corollary to this delineation of a pedagogic Arcadia. Granted status, salary and conditions of this ilk, then one might have the right to expect that the teachers recruited would have some element in their training to distinguish them as suitable for the task and its appropriate benefits. One must reiterate the claim for pre-service options (and in-service refresher courses). These latter might, of course, best be organized by LEAs on a part-time basis of, for example, a day a week over a year, with the occasional week-end conference. College teams could help cover one or two such absentees so that, over a five or seven year phase, practically all staff might have this opportunity. Fulltime half-term courses and even holiday and correspondence courses might play a part. These courses would aim at ensuring a respectable competence in handling EPA teaching problems, particularly in reference to the newer theory and practice promulgated in recent years. It might be anticipated that such courses would constitute eligibility, after the five or seven year moratorium, for the rewards of EPA teaching – until that juncture, of course, the present teaching personnel would automatically be eligible.

The enlargement of the EPA concept and the improvement of EPA teacher status would be a superficially costly investment, but, in the longterm, the social and educational benefits could be immense. It would assuredly be the necessary climate in which a project team, described earlier in this chapter, could work most effectively. Costing for these project groups is well nigh impossible. The establishment and administrative maintenance of such a team might cost anything from £20,000 to £40,000 a year according to size. For centralized roles (pre-school support, teacher-resources, publications, training) costs might be roughly estimated at between £5,000 and £20,000 a year according to aim. For individualized efforts both in primary and secondary schools one might add the £150 or 50p. per capita public relations grant already mentioned to a further similar sum for other activities. On average, this might (recalling the larger sizes of secondary, as opposed to primary, schools) mean a total of

£500. One might then argue a pattern of forty schools to a project unit (either under the aegis of one large LEA or several small ones) which would suggest a sum for school action of £20,000. In total, then, a project might annually be budgetted at between £45,000 and £80,000, but this, it is re-emphasized, is arithmetic in part by guess work. These are not exorbitant amounts and yet they could embrace through the media of project teams, the whole breadth of recommendations here outlined.

Whatever else, personnel and resources must be released to implement, if they are accepted, the proposals, developed from the Liverpool project, on a national basis and it is scarcely contestable that the most productive way of allocating these would be in rational units, such as project teams, rather than in random dribs and drabs of an appointment here and a release of monies there.

It is hoped that, by these means or by more conventional DES or LEA techniques, a large-scale EPA community education programme will be implemented. It is partially in this hope that we decided independently to establish a national centre in Liverpool for EPA work, to be called 'Priority'. This centre has a number of functions. It endeavours to maintain and extend the actual Liverpool Project as a demonstration of urban community schooling; it acts as a coordination information centre for like work on a national scale; it publishes a thrice-yearly journal *Priority News*,* and various books, reports and occasional papers; it will continue to produce prototype kits and other materials; and to offer a training service to those who feel in need of its support; it will attempt to float innovations and research probes up and down the country; it will take into account a full spectrum of need, from pre-school to adult education and in-including industry, theatre and all other aspects of community life; it will attempt to involve the popular media, such as the press and television in community education; it will try, with its Speakers' Panels, by conferences, courses and other means, to build up an audience for urban community schooling; in general, it will aim at keeping alive an enlarged and profound

* 'Priority News' is published in January, May and September. It costs 10p. a copy and postal subscribers should send 40p. (10p. each copy and 10p. postage) to Richard Blake, ACE, 32 Trumpington St., Cambridge.

concept of the EPA problem and a vigorous and positive portrayal of its resolution.

With great foresight and wisdom, the Liverpool LEA has kindly given us the material wherewithal and full encouragement to establish our Centre in its midst, and, of course, their assistance is indispensable. The Social and Administrative Studies Department at Oxford – the original national base for the EPA Project – the Advisory Centre for Education at Cambridge, the Liverpool Council of Social Services, the pick of the Liverpool Colleges, Merseyside business interests, including splendid support from John Moores Junior, and several other individuals and agencies, have promised vital support. The Centre began operations in January 1972 with a basic team of six, comfortably ensconced in our new home at the Harrison Jones School, with accommodation, equipment, furnishings and office services generously provided by the Liverpool authority.

This would seem an admirable consummation of an action-research scheme. On the one hand, a Report and Recommendations have been presented to mark the end of the initial project. On the other hand, this action-research project took on an organic embodiment of its own and, from its Liverpool core, it developed a national perspective. In a sense, the Centre is a report-in-practice and it seems right that a substantially action-oriented programme should so record itself.

These, then, are some interim conclusions and thoughts drawn from three years' action-research in Liverpool. It has been none too soon to lay down guide-lines, bitty and haphazard although they might appear, for a national EPA policy. Sometimes we are told the Project should have lasted ten years in order to make really convincing proposals. This surely misses the point that it is a question of urgency, that, whereas (as the Plowden Report implied) all schools should be 'community schools', the Community School might be a matter of life and death for the EPAs and that an educational policy of 'constructive discontent' might well be earnestly required to avoid the possible alternative of blind rebellion. In these circumstances, time is a factor in the game; we must produce the optimal policy given those circumstances. We are in the position of the examination candidate who knows that he hasn't enough time to do himself justice, but that the challenge is to produce four answers against three hours on the clock. Indeed, so pressing is the need, both for the practical purpose of avoiding pronounced social dislocation and for the moral purpose of ensuring an elementary system of social justice, that it would have been preferable to have come up with an answer in three weeks.

8 The Future
Too Little, Too Late?

It must be emphasized that the establishment of the EPA Community School is not, of itself, an answer to the problem of multideprivation. Simply, it would be of not much use for the school to turn out a beautifully balanced product, if the scope to enjoy work, leisure and other social amenities did not exist. Community Education must, then, be seen essentially as an element in the spectrum of Community Development, alongside employment patterns, housing, police, welfare and every other social and economic service agency, otherwise it would be merely tinkering to reappraise the school in vacuo. Nonetheless, education may lay some claim to be primus inter pares. It is worth noting that the Home Office Community Development Projects have approached us for advice in the Community Education field, and I am happy to act as Educational Consultant for them. The alert organizers of these ambitious programmes have been quick to realize that the school has often the highest common multiple of community concern – everyone has been to school; many have children at or approaching school age; most live near a school. It could be said that if communal togetherness cannot be founded in a common concern for children then the prospects are indeed dreary.

In the longer term, the school is probably the soundest bet for an investment in community regeneration. If the Community School, with a community-oriented content and treatment, can help breed generations of children to react imaginatively, briskly and articulately to the problems of social disadvantage and redevelopment, then the whole gamut of community action would be substantially improved. One is not euphoric about this. It is not a dewy-eyed vision; rather is it a pessimistic warning that this may be one of the only possible alternatives to the negative and destructive collision course upon which many of our urban areas seem set.

The regeneration of community life in Educational Priority Areas and in the redevelopment areas which they become or to which their inhabitants are drafted – this is the overriding objective of EPA Community Education. There are short-term pay-offs – a probable improvement in traditional attainments, given a relevant approach; a heightening of parental interest via more realistic content; a more stable school/community relation and so forth – but these must be seen as subsidiary to the idyll of urban renaissance. It is this dimension of Community Education which takes it a large step past the vogue reverence for Compensatory Education. Basically, Compensatory Education is concerned with the individual who has school potential that, in happier social conditions, would be realized. It is a case of to each according to his educational *ability*. Community Education recognizes that, whatever the dispensation, the majority of EPA and redevelopment children will eke out their lives in such localities, and it is with these localities that they have to come to terms. It is not opposed to (by and large, it welcomes) 'compensation'; but it goes beyond it. It is a case of to each according to his educational *need*.

It will be noticed that the twilight zones and the municipal estates have been lumped together in this analysis, purely on the grounds that the latter is the (sometimes) physically improved outcome of the former. But, overall, the requirements of a healthy community fabric for both are very similar. How is one, in fact, to achieve self-generating, participatory communal solidity in these situations, where, in flesh and spirit, a 'we' and 'them' dichotomy exists? It may be true that the middle-class suburbs and the commuter villages also lack identity and purpose and that, always assumming grass-roots democracy is an acceptable goal to pursue, it behoves the State and its local governmental entities to tackle the question of community development wholesale.

Although there is a risk of spotting and selecting evidence, there does seem to be a ground swell towards local and individual political activity. This can be seen in the crop of consumer-type pressure groups and associations, in such fields as retail trading, education and land utilization and of various forms of tenant and resident bodies. Sometimes, these are continuing agencies; sometimes, they come together temporarily to fight a specific cause, such as comprehensive education or the siting of an airfield. The phenomenon of the 'demonstration' has become much more common and has manifested itself in the most conventional and genteel walks of life. Nor has trades union militancy slackened unduly, with the strike and now the work-in in frequent use. A dramatic illustration has been at the student level, where political and social activism and commitment has been very pronounced. Throughout Europe and the United States a wide range of anti-establishment and extra-state movements has come into being, normally based on a locality or a minority feeling aggrieved at the action or inaction of authority. One must not exaggerate this. It is not new. It is not total and one must know where to look to find it. It is brought into being because the State remains strong and because alongside it, a heavy pressure of public and private corporations weigh upon the individual.

Such activities have their visionary side, but they are neither theoretically synthetic nor hyperbolically futuristic. After all, consumer, tenant, trades union, parent-teacher and many other associations do actually exist and the feeling for locality is often strong and deep-rooted. It is admittedly, an emotive, even a sentimental, proposition. Therein lies its strength. It would see a demolished house as a shattered home and might not examine the wholesale removal of people under a cold and abstract heading like 'decantation'. Beyond that, it would throw down the democratic gauntlet. Do we or do we not want a thoroughgoing participatory democracy? Are we frightened of giving power to the people and are the people frightened of accepting power?

A tentative beginning has been made and should be sustained. In a city like Liverpool, there is an excitement in the political air about community development. It is a city with a gritty heritage of compact community life and yet with a cosmopolitan atmosphere of vigour and good cheer. The encouraging Shelter Neighbourhood Action Plan (SNAP) with its far-reaching plan for a Granby area 'new town' in the city centre and the equally promising Home Office Community Development Project (CDP) for the Vauxhall locality both offered splendid opportunities for major pilot programmes. An active Neighbourhood Organizations Committee, a series of strong Community Councils and Area Community Wardens and a wide range of other excellent resources exists. The local authority are sympathetic and sensitive to the mood, at both officer and elective levels, and are diligently trying to define a Community Development policy and a corresponding structure. It might be that Liverpool could become the nodal point for a massive experiment of this kind.

Optimistically, one might look forward to the purpose-built community. One of the difficulties of formulating the Community School as a physical entity is the temptation to see it as the core, rather than as an element, in the community. One, too naïvely, visualizes the school as a centripetal agency with radial spokes to other social and economic peripheries. If the school is to be in and of the community, then, ideally, this philosophic attitude should be physically transcribed. One should imagine the pram-park for the shopping precinct running into the pre-school unit; the school clinic as part of the group surgery; the school library as a section of the branch library; a total sharing of recreational and leisure facilities; the school dining-room gelled in with the civic café or restaurant; and so on in a fluid and flexible format. The motto: to be in school is to be in the community; to be in the community is to be in school. One could note examples of this social fluency in regard to other institutions and extend the hypothesis to the economy as well.

A policy of communal comprehensiveness is an attempt to find a golden mean between the remoteness of highly efficacious economies of scale and the negation of order, the social chaos and violence, that threatens our urban centres. Not that the former is so very marvellous. It cannot be too often recalled that some of the most disastrous social problems of the age have been the consequence not of accident nor of neglect but of design. It is with an effort of mind that one looks at some high-rise blocks and remembers that they were done on purpose. Alternatively, few of us would welcome the appalling anarchy and destruction of extreme social breakdown. The disadvantages of the artificially erected commune in a social vacuum are lack of resources and services; the disadvantages of the monolithic authority is its divorcement from the community. A federal formula of large providing and small deciding authorities might just attain the best of both worlds.

It is interesting to study whether any rewarding models exist. A self-educated working-man, writing under the pseudonym, 'A Liverpool Shipwright', in the Liverpool journal *Porcupine* in 1877, commented that schooling needed 'an educational Rowland Hill' to run it on the same basis as the GPO. It is a fascinating thought. Although its image has recently become a little tarnished, the Post Office has, for over a century, managed normally to combine the massive with the minute, with an international telecommunications service at one pole and the friendly neighbourhood postman and the old age pension from the corner shop at the other pole. The BBC, now that is is engaged in local radio with some local governance, or the Co-operative Wholesale Society, or the National Health Service all have elements that might be cited as other examples. To take the schools again as an instance, there could perhaps be a national Educational Corporation which would be ready and equipped to modify, renew or create educational institutions to the remits of the consumer groups. And a Housing Corporation and a Libraries Corporation and a Welfare Corporation and the rest. These would be servants, not masters, prepared to provide and maintain at the behest of the client populations, who would, in turn, ensure a balance and interdependence of action within their ambit. Needless to say, this is not a blueprint; it is a guideline. It is a radical one, but only because it is a desperate situation. There would be a thousand objections from a hundred directions. One age-old grumble would be dredged up, namely, the people couldn't or wouldn't be able to handle the issues. Thus, the argument comes full circle. The most telling answer to this criticism would be to go all-out for a gigantic programme of Community Education that children be equipped, over succeeding generations, to make a nonsense of this complaint. There is the rub. Community Education would be futile and wasteful outside a comprehensive policy of Community Development; Community Development would be inhibited and emasculated without a thoroughgoing exercise in Community Education.

The thoughts and practices of the community educator and the community developer meet those of the conservationists, the doomwatch prophets, the ecologists, the military strategists, the population experts and all those who express concern about the future of man and, especially, urban man. It is a gloomy prospect, and the urban community developer mounts a formidable case as he asks for social justice for the inhabitants of our deprived, along with an urgent warning about the likelihood of urban collapse and degeneration, with its self-evident repercussions throughout all society. Optimism and pessimism mingle. My optimism has risen these last four years as I have watched teachers, parents, children and others respond splendidly to Community School promptings. My pessimism has also risen during the same period, as the problem has accumulated so much faster than either the awareness has been sharpened or the solutions have been pressed. In other words, granted the radical change of attitudes, the total commitment to urban reappraisal and the huge in-put of necessary resources, we could outwit the futurologists and invent our own destiny. But we are very probably doing too little too late.

One hates to talk arithmetically about the future, but an estimate, not in strictly calculated temporal terms, so much as in an attempt to offer an order of magnitude, may give some idea of perspective. My own considered opinion is that, at the present rate of development, we might expect a complete regeneration of urban life in something like fifty to a hundred years. But we may have only fifteen or twenty years in which to accomplish this challenging feat of urban salvage.